♥ FREE BONUS

Would you LOVE to learn one new skill that will help you achive nearly all your results?

Get all the resources needed for this book. It's FREE and updated regularly at:

HernaniAlves.com/Bonus

SCAN with Phone

Here is what you'll receive...

- Top 20 Balanced Accountability Assessment
- Personal Report Card
- Personal Engagement Survey For Feedback
- Leadership Love Language
- Six Steps to Address the Energy Vampire
- S.M.A.R.T. Mentoring Form
- Playbook to Peer-to-Peer Accountability
- And a few surprises along the way....

♥ Praise for **Balanced Accountability**

"Hernani's work on Balanced Accountability drives every aspect of an organization's success. Here is a roadmap helping to create high performance organizations. Having clear accountability is a crucial element to bring out the best in people and help drive your company to exceptional business success."
—**Dr. Robert L Lorber**, CEO of The Lorber Kamai Consulting Group, Co-author *Putting The One Minute Manager To Work* with **Ken Blanchard**

♥

"True accountability isn't a punishment to employ when things go awry; when practiced with balance and love, it's a way to unleash peak performance in ourselves and others. And, lucky for us, Hernani Alves lays out the principles and method for doing just that. Balanced Accountability should be required reading for every manager and entrepreneur."
—**Steve Farber**, Founder, The Extreme Leadership Institute; author, *The Radical LEAP, Greater Than Yourself,* and *Love Is Just Damn Good Business*

♥

"Commitment is at the core of successful entrepreneurial ventures and remains paramount in every meaningful personal relationship. If you want to be a leader and make a deep impact on the world, a great start is with Balanced Accountability. This book will give you the tools to lead your team and create a high performing culture. Hernani shares his touching and insightful story while shedding light on real-world business challenges."
—**Mark Haney**, Founder of Haney Business Ventures, *Mark Haney Radio Show* and Allegiant Giving Charitable Organization which Invests in Combat Wounded Veterans.

"Hernani does an excellent job of defining the balance of culture in your organization while driving the results needed by holding your team members accountable. Great read for those leaders that need a boost and reminder that a strong balanced culture is the foundation of success."
—**Sara McClure**, President, *iHeart Media*, Sacramento Market

♥

"I have had the honor and pleasure of working with Hernani for more than a dozen years, and I find him to be an incredibly talented, humble, and gifted leader. He holds himself to a high degree of accountability and integrity, so he speaks from experience from the heart. He inspires through his actions as much as with words. These Balanced Accountability skills are critical in being a successful business leader."
—**Tracy Jackson**, EVP, Chief Human Resource Officer,
Safe Credit Union

♥

"If you want to be a leader and make a deep impact on the world, a great start is with Balanced Accountability. This book will give you the tools to lead your team and create a high performing culture."
—**Vlad Skots**, Founder/CEO, *USKO Express*

♥

"One of the most honest and heart-felt books I've ever read on how to build and lead a team. Inspiring, audacious, but with a down-home feel and with a big splash of getting comfortable with that 'naughty word' accountability. Bravo Mr. Alves for giving us a book about self-awareness, building relationships, and family, both at home and at work, and how the loving and serving them all is really the key to becoming better leaders in every way."
—**Indie Bollman**, MBA, SHRM-SCP, SPHR, Director of Corporate
Development, *Trailer Bridge*

"Balanced Accountability is an exceptional guide to help you learn to be an effective leader, coach, and mentor utilizing accountability to create incredibly high performing teams. Hernani will entertain you with relatable examples, his personal journey as a padawan learner, and share his unique guide of how to become a loved and respected leader."

—**Matt Jessell**, Founder of *Jessell Business Consulting*, COO of *Telesis Construction Inc.*

♥

"Balanced Accountability works, and I've witnessed his process firsthand. Having worked with Hernani for the better part of two decades, I have seen the results from his High Performing teams. I highly recommend you learn from his vast experience and success with Balanced Accountability."

—**Scott Higgins** – Regional Vice President of Sales, *Mattress Firm*

♥

"I learned lessons in Leadership and Accountability from Hernani more than a decade ago that I still employ to this day. If you truly care about how well someone will perform, hold them accountable and challenge them to be their best version of themself!"

—**Brendan McGagin**, MBA, Regional Vice President of Sales, *Mattress Firm*

♥

"Balanced Accountability is a must-read for all leaders, no matter the stage of your career. Hernani's framework for accountability delivers both the vision and the guidance for cultivating a high performance team. The application of the 3Ps will have a positive impact on your growth and development not only as a leader, but as a person."

—**Tammy Dudek**, Communications Manager, *Mattress Firm*

Balanced Accountability

Three Leadership Secrets To
Win Hearts And
Maximize Performance

Hernani Alves

Balanced IQ
Leadership

Balanced Accountability
3 Leadership Secrets to Win Hearts & Maximize Performance
By Hernani Alves

Published by: Balanced IQ Leadership,
8814 Fiador Court, Roseville, CA 95747, USA.
www.BalancedIQ.com
Cover Design: Pedrag Capo

Ordering Information:
Balanced IQ offers excellent discounts on this book when ordered in quantity for bulk purchases or special sales. For more information, please contact Hernani.Alves@BalancedIQ.com.

ISBN-13: 978-1-7337791-0-4   Hardback
ISBN-10: 1-7337791-0-8

ISBN-13: 978-1-7337791-1-1   Paperback
ISBN-10: 1-7337791-1-6

Library of Congress Control Number: 2019936666
(hardback) 1. Leadership. 2. Accountability in personnel management. 3. Communication. 4. Organizational Change
I. Title

www.HernaniAlves.com

*To my parents, **Antonio** and **Maria**,*
for showing me unconditional love and
holding me accountable.

Contents

Dale Carlsen

Founder and CEO of Sleep Train, and
CEO and Chairman of the Board for Ticket to Dream

"If you want to be successful, surround yourself with great people, treat them well and make everyone successful." When I opened my first Sleep Train store in 1985, my dad gave me this great piece of advice; I took my dad's words to heart and was very blessed to be surrounded by a team of incredible leaders. Hernani Alves not only was one of these leaders, but he also went on to lead Sleep Train as President and became a top leader in Mattress Firm, a $3 billion company, after our sale to them. I was proud to see him at the helm of Sleep Train and knew he would bring great value to Mattress Firm.

Prior to meeting Hernani, I kept overhearing my team talk about an employee who worked for us down in the Stockton/Modesto market who apparently had "a nanny." They would say her nanny this or her nanny that. Finally, one day I asked, "Who has a nanny?" They all laughed and said the employee's name was Hernani—pronounced her nanny—and he was doing some amazing numbers.

Hernani could sell anyone and, over the early years as he grew, I could see his leadership skills grow as well. Hernani believes, as I do, in accountability and the need to get everyone aligned with the company's goals and objectives. Looking to maximize his potential both for himself and our growing company, I approached Hernani and asked him to step out of sales, where he was having great success, to help us train our team. From this point on, Hernani, who always wanted to improve himself and those around him, grew as a true leader at Sleep Train. He brought his high integrity, insistence on accountability, family values—and as you will learn later, and his love to all those who worked with him.

Now, don't get me wrong, Hernani and I did not always see eye to eye. Hernani was one of those young leaders who believed it was easier to get forgiveness rather than permission. As part of our leadership team, he would constantly challenge me and rapidly became the top person to trigger my classic "red face." Being of Danish descent, my fair skin shows my emotions and turns red when I am frustrated. Hernani would often "be proactive" (in his words) and push the envelope of policies when he felt it was in the best interest of the company. This would result in him and I having many discussions where we would share each other's "opinions." As time went on, we became more in sync as I gained trust in his motives and Hernani learned to make changes in a less disruptive manner, through a culture of love and accountability.

High Performance Culture

If you are looking to build a high-performance culture with true accountability, you will want to read this book and discover how to integrate Hernani's 3Ps of accountability into your organization and understand that LOVE should not be a four-letter word in a company that truly wants to achieve great things. As my dad told me and Hernani and my team have proven, if you surround yourself with great people, treat them well and make everyone successful, you will achieve your goals beyond what you thought possible. I wish you the best. Enjoy the book!

[1]

ACCOUNTABILITY: THE NAUGHTY WORD

"If you want to live a life you've never lived, you have to do things you've never done."

—Jen Sincero, author of *You Are a Badass: How to Stop Doubting Your Greatness and Start Living an Awesome Life.*

Cow Number One was a special cow. She was, as the number suggests, the first calf ever born on our farm. We started the dairy farm after my family emigrated from Africa to America. Desperate for a better life, my parents dragged their four young kids out of civil war in Angola to a refugee camp, to the Azores Islands—my father's original homeland, and eventually on to the United States.

In our new country, Dad started a fish market, successfully sold it, and (for reasons I don't quite understand) decided dairy farming was the easiest path to a better life. The sprawling farmlands of Idaho promised low start-up costs for a new dairy business, so Jerome, Idaho was where we ended up.

By the time Cow Number One was all grown up, I was a scrawny nine-year-old, 75 pounds soaking wet and, despite my lacking strength, expected to do my part on the farm. At that age, that meant milking the cows after school. I'll never forget the first time I tried to milk Cow Number One.

She'd just had her calf and had never been in the milking barn before. It was a cold day, and I could see my breath as I called her over. My numb hands fumbled with the bag as I poured out grain to tempt her into the holding pen, but she wasn't into it. She kicked and kicked, throwing her 1,500 pounds of weight around the barn. She got scared and ice-cold manure flew everywhere, primarily on me.

I wanted to calm her, tried again to give her grain, but she was running crazy. I just couldn't wrestle that milking machine on her. I was cold, hungry, covered in manure, and kind of fed up. So I opened the gate, let her go and began cleaning up.

A few minutes later, I heard the gate open behind me. I turned and saw Cow Number One stomping back in, followed by my dad. My dad was a solid, straight-backed man. He was in farm shape, strong and muscular with hands rough like sandpaper. As a kid, I thought his fingers were made from pure muscle; they were so firm and strong.

His was the most rigid handshake I ever experienced. He wasn't—still isn't—a man of many words, and I knew, without him saying a thing, that I was in for it.

You see, when you don't milk a cow, she can get an infection called mastitis. Then you have to put penicillin in her, you can't sell the milk, and you just have to hope it cures. Plus, this first milking was supposed to feed Cow Number One's new calf. The milk contained protective antibodies that would keep the baby healthy and strong. I could've killed the calf by robbing her of that valuable milk.

But I was a kid and didn't care about that. I just wanted to go home, sit by the fire, and eat a warm, home cooked dinner.

My dad was furious I hadn't milked Cow Number One. He gave me the biggest spanking of my life. It was intense, so much so that I peed my pants. I cried. I wanted to run home to mom. It was something I'd never do to my children.

When he was done, he had me put a device on the cow to hold her hips and stop her kicking. He made me milk her. He made me finish the job.

My Dad Held Me Accountable

For years, I hated him for that moment, but I always knew he loved me. It was this experience, more than any other, that taught me that love and accountability are intertwined. We'll talk more about why that is in the next chapter. Once I understood that my dad held me accountable because he loved me, because he wanted to teach me to do the job right the first time and finish what

I started, to set me up with a work ethic that would help me be successful in life, all my thoughts about accountability—in life and in business—started to fall into place.

It took me many years to work through those ideas, but as I did, I became more loving toward my parents. I morphed into a better leader in the workplace, and I formed the basis of the life-changing leadership model you'll learn in this book.

That model helped me rise through the ranks at work from a part-time salesperson while at college to eventually becoming president of the company. As I rose, I was given the incredible opportunity to speak at some of our company conferences. One of these was at L.A. LIVE, a gathering of over five thousand of our junior and executive leaders at the stunning JW Marriott in downtown L.A.

We were camped out in the huge conference center, a sweeping stage at the front, giant projector screens around the room showing close-ups of the speakers captured by a professional film crew, and ambient lighting setting an upbeat mood. We'd spent two days listening to company execs celebrating our wins and inspiring us for the busy selling season that was almost upon us. Now it was my turn.

My parents were sat in the front row. I had my sister, Fatima, and brother-in-law, Frank, bring them along, saying I was to be presented with a surprise award and the company wanted them there to witness my moment.

That was a lie.

In fact, I was going to present them with an award.

I jumped up on stage and thanked the previous presenter. I'd been asked to speak on "stubborn leadership," but instead of starting with business or teams or management styles, I launched into the story of my father's life. I talked about how he stubbornly sought opportunities, even when none seemed nearby. I told the audience how he led his family from country to country, determined to create something better for himself and, in doing so, made a wonderful life for his family.

I invited him and my mom onto the stage and presented them with an award for Best Parents Within The Alves Family. I publicly thanked my parents for everything they'd done for my siblings and me, and for the incredible example they'd set for my wife, Angie, and I as we raised our own children. It was an award well-earned and one that I hope to win someday from my children.

Parenting Requires You Hold Your Kids Accountable

It's no coincidence that my dad was a fantastic father and had a strong sense of accountability. That understanding of accountability was integral to his parenting. This is something we've all experienced as parents or watching others with their kids.

Parents have to hold their children accountable for their actions. If your son hits another child, when he knows hitting is wrong, you'll quickly address the situation. You'll hold him accountable for his actions. If he keeps being a bully, there'll be consequences. You'll take away his toy or give him a timeout. Pretty standard, right?

I've come a long way since that scrawny nine-year-old. I have my own children now. My daughter, Carmina, is 15 and my son, Riley, is 11. As responsible parents, my wonderful wife and I have to hold them accountable for their behavior.

They're old enough to know there are some four-letter words we don't say. There are the obvious ones, you know, and a few extras unique to our house. One of those is "fair." We got sick of hearing, "That's not fair," so banned the word.

Now, if anyone says it, they have to drop and do ten push-ups. I hold my kids accountable to this rule. Riley once got stubborn and ended up doing seventy push-ups in a row. One time he busted me while ranting about politics, and I had to do 10 push-ups. My wife's done them, too. We hold each other accountable, and it's a good thing. We're all better, less whiny people for it.

The Naughty Word

But in the workplace, holding others accountable isn't seen as a good thing. Even the word itself is seen as naughty; it's whispered or avoided entirely. Do you hear it discussed in your office?

Most people don't, or they hear it in a really negative context. The Workplace Accountability Study, which looked at more than forty thousand participants over multiple years and across many industries, said, "there is an accountability crisis in organizations today, and it is a crisis of epidemic proportions."

Its research showed "overwhelming" evidence that people perceive accountability to be something that happens when things go wrong, instead of a tool to encourage improved results. This misunderstanding is at the heart of many workplace problems.

If you have high turnover in your team, if your employees are regularly missing sales targets, or just aren't engaged, it's because you're not harnessing the power of effective accountability in your leadership. That might be hard for you to hear, and it was initially a struggle for me. It really is the crux of workplace problems, though, both big and small.

Does it drive you crazy when...

- Your team doesn't read your emails?
- You have to repeat yourself time and time again?
- Employees miss deadlines?
- You get stonewalled in meetings, your team just sitting there with blank faces, not offering any feedback?

Trouble recruiting, poor customer service, and lack of employee engagement are all common problems in offices across the world. They're all signs that the person in charge is managing, not leading.

Managers Versus Leaders

Before I understood the difference, I wanted to be a manager. While in college, I got a part-time sales job for a mattress retailer. I got the sales bug and aspired to climb the corporate ranks. I worked hard, exceeded my sales targets, and took my first step up that ladder to become a store manager.

Manager... I was thrilled. I got off to a great start. In my first two months, I tripled the store's previous sales volume. Although my sales figures exceeded all expectations, I soon saw those problems I mentioned above and many more. It got so bad my employees nicknamed me after one of the evilest men in history.

In the next chapter, I'll tell you that story, and how I overcame my own faults to become executive vice-president of a $3 billion company and received a Best Leader award from my team—my most cherished accolade. It's the story of how I stopped managing and started leading, using accountability to improve every aspect of my team.

Make a Commitment

But before we get to that story, I want you to make a commitment to yourself. You picked up this book because things aren't as good as they could be at work, but you want it to improve. You're in a difficult situation, managing multiple personalities in a busy workplace, with constant challenges being thrown at you. It isn't easy.

But using the processes you'll learn in this book, you can turn things around. You'll see real changes in your organization. You and your team will perform better and see more success than ever before. In turn, you'll have less stress, feel more accomplished, and give those same benefits to your employees.

So commit to reading this book all the way through and acting on its advice. It's all tested, proven action that will make a difference to your work. You won't have to do this alone; I'll guide you through each step. You do have to take action, though.

You should, right? You owe it to yourself to try. Remember Jen Sincero's quote from the beginning of this chapter: "If you want to live a life you've never lived, you have to do things you've never done."

♥ Take Action

Throughout this book, we'll end each chapter with a few questions to ask yourself, and some action items so you can take solid steps toward your goal of a well-functioning workplace. You can keep your answers private or share them with me at Hernani.Alves@BalancedIQ.com. I'd love to hear how you're doing.

1. Will you commit to reading this book all the way through and acting on its advice? Download the FREE resources for this book at: HernaniAlves.com/Bonus

2. How do you use accountability outside of work? Think about your family, friends, and hobbies.

3. Write a thank you letter or, better yet, call and thank that special someone in your life who has taught you about accountability, as my parents did for me. You'll make their day and you'll feel great for telling them.

[2]

A SUCCESS STORY

"Accountability breeds response-ability."

—Stephen R. Covey, author of The 7 Habits of Highly
Effective People: Powerful Lessons in Personal Change.

My dad wasn't just a fish market manager and dairy
farmer. He was, in fact, a serial entrepreneur who taught
me my first business—and life—lessons. He was born in the
Azores Islands, which are halfway between New York and
Portugal. His island, Sao Jorge, was just four miles wide by
27 miles long, and there weren't many opportunities there.
When dad was 18, he would look out over the water and
think, There must be more to life than this.

It was the 1950s and Angola, in southern Africa, was
prospering with diamond mining. So dad saved his money
and persuaded a stranger to sell him their ticket for the

fully-booked boat to Lobito, Angola. The journey took two months, and when he arrived, he had nowhere to go. There was no Google, no Yelp, and he didn't speak the language. He was homeless for two weeks and ate scrap food before finding a job at a trading post.

People would bring eggs, milk, whatever they had from their farm, and barter for what they needed. It was essentially a sales job, and dad became the top salesman. He loved it and, at 21 years old, summoned his courage and asked the owner to help him open his own store. The owner gave him a credit limit and soon, the new store was up and running.

It wasn't easy. Dad would take anything as payment; quilts, pigs, chickens, whatever it took to sell something. But he never gave up. He met and married my mom, who joined him in the business. Over the years, they opened two trading posts, then two auto body shops, and an auto parts store. They went from poverty to the upper classes. They bought a big house, filled it with nice things, and lived a good life. They had my older sister, my two brothers, and, in June of 1975, my mom gave birth to me.

That year, 1975, is burned into the collective memory of all Angolans. It was the year the civil war started. No one knew it then, but that war would last 27 years and take the lives of more than five hundred thousand people. Over one million people would be displaced, and we were to be among them.

Losing Everything

I was three months old when it happened. It was early morning. Mom was preparing breakfast, and there was a knock on the door of the house like you've never heard. It was a knock to scare you. It happened again. It was loud. It was aggressive. Dad thought, Is this a threat? Do I open the door?

He took a chance, unlocked the door, and peered out. The neighbor stood on the doorstep looking frantic. He shouted at my dad, "Get out! Get out! The guerrilla army is coming. They're going to kill you. Leave, now." My dad grabbed the kids, his wife, and a bottle of milk for the baby—me, and got out of there.

He and my mom found a Red Cross refugee camp in South Africa. Thank god for the Red Cross. But it was tough there. It was overpopulated. People would fight for bread and scavenge scraps of food from the dirt to feed their kids. Our family survived and, after six months, were able to escape. A lot of people didn't. Some had so much stress they had heart attacks. Others couldn't deal with everything they'd lost, and killed themselves.

Finding Success, Again

My parents had lost everything, too. But, being the entrepreneur he was, dad started again. Back in the Azores Islands, he opened a restaurant. He did well but still wanted a better life for his children. He brought us to the States, started that fish market, then the dairy farm, and provided comfort and countless opportunities for me, my sister, and my brothers, including my younger brother who was born in Idaho.

I grew up hearing this story, and it gave me profound confidence that success is possible for anyone, in any circumstances. So when I was 23 and got a part-time job at a mattress store called Sleep Train, in Modesto, California, I assumed I would be successful there. And I was. I loved the buzz, the adrenaline that came with making a sale. While still in college, I went full-time and, six months later, was managing my own store in Stockton, California.

It wasn't a flashy store. It was in a rough part of town, and the company rumor-mill declared it was cursed. The day after it opened, it had caught on fire. The staff there were miserable, sales were lousy, and, as far as careers were concerned, it was where you went to die. But I went in determined to succeed. I started from scratch and did it all by the book. I paid attention to everything, grilling the team on how to serve customers to the correct way to vacuum the store, to exactly when and how to take out the trash.

A Little Success and a Big Problem

After two months, we were breaking sales records. On the sales report, I could see our store going from the bottom of the pack to passing up above some high-performing stores. I thought we were on the path to success.

But that was when I heard the nickname the team used behind my back.

Instead of Hernani, they called me Hernazi.

They had decided I was a Nazi. They put me on par with the worst people of all time. I couldn't believe it. We were getting results, but no one wanted to work with the Nazi. I was distraught at learning what they really thought of me, and wondered how I'd gone so wrong.

Because of the success I'd had on paper, I'd won the company's Presidents Club Trip—an all-expenses paid vacation to Maui, Hawaii. At the airport bookstore, I trawled through the business books, searching for help. I picked up *Whale Done: The Power of Positive Relationships* by Ken Blanchard. It teaches leaders how to magnify positives at work and focus on doing things right.

Reading that book, I realized my employees weren't just being mean for no reason; I was a big problem. People didn't want to work with me because I was micromanaging and refusing to give positive reinforcement.

Small Praises, Small Steps

When I returned to the store, I put into practice the lessons from Whale Done. I started praising my staff for small things, like greeting a guest well or taking the trash out early. Even when they didn't get quite the right result, if it was a step in the right direction, I praised them. I started to buy them meals when we exceeded our sales targets. Then I encouraged them to invite a guest and saw how proud they were to celebrate with their spouse or a friend.

Small step followed small step, and the store improved faster than ever. Before finding out what my team really thought of me, I'd always considered myself a good boss because I got consistently strong sales numbers. But now, "boss" became my second least-favorite word. (I'll tell you my least favorite word in chapter five.)

I learned real success doesn't come from bossing your employees around. And it doesn't come from "managing" people. No one likes to be managed. A manager is a whip, a stick, a Hernazi. But everything changes when you stop being a boss or a manager and start being a leader. Leaders guide their employees to success. They inspire. They encourage creativity. It's a different mindset, and it gives different results.

Finding Success for Myself and Others

I went on to lead bigger departments and mentor many employees—even some who weren't my direct reports but who went out of their way to work with me. In 2014, Mattress Firm paid $425 million to acquire Sleep Train and Dale, our founder (who wrote the foreword to this book), gave 25 percent of that to our employees. I was appointed president of Sleep Train and, as part of Mattress Firm, we evolved into a brand worth over $3 billion, with over 3,500 locations throughout the United States, and more than 15,000 fantastic employees. I loved my work, and I loved the people I worked with. Much of my success was due to those people—a high-performing team who taught me the power of accountability. Their wisdom, experience, and honesty helped me learn the lessons I'll share with you in this book.

In 2017, we converted Sleep Train to Mattress Firm, and I left to become the founder and Chief Executive Officer of Balanced IQ, a leadership consulting business. I help leaders motivate the hearts of their teams to maximize their company's results. I teach them the techniques I used to turn my business and life around so they can turn their underperforming teams into sales superstars. Throughout my career, I've used these strategies with everyone from 16-year-olds in their first part-time job, to high-performing sales executives—many of whom I mentor to this very day. Time and time again, their success has blown me away.

The 3Ps

As I zoned in on the techniques that really worked, I distilled them into a program I call The 3Ps. I worked with human resource professionals who were eager for more people to understand the 3Ps. They challenged me, tested the processes, and helped me improve. I owe thanks in particular to Tracy Jackson, the incredible human resource (HR) professional I worked with Sleep Train. She taught me that we must focus on the human part of HR. As we go through this book and the 3Ps program, you'll see that it's all about being human.

But before I tell you what the 3Ps are, we need to talk about a concept you might find uncomfortable. We're going to talk about love. It's a weird conversation to have in the workplace but, as you'll see, success comes from accountability, and accountability is all about love.

♥ Take Action

1. What has been your own journey to this point of your career, and what have you learned doesn't work in leadership?

2. How has your family and environment affected your thoughts around success? How has it influenced your ideas on accountability?

3. Write a list of anything that makes you feel uncomfortable as you consider accountability.

[3]

ACCOUNTABILITY = LOVE

"I don't necessarily have to like my players and associates but as their leader I must love them.

Love is loyalty, love is teamwork, love respects the dignity of the individual.

This is the strength of any organization."

—Vince Lombardi, former NFL coach for whom the Super Bowl trophy was named after.

Vince Lombardi was one of the most successful National Football League (NFL) coaches in history. Unfortunately, it wasn't my team—the San Francisco 49ers—that he helped to victory. For most of his career, Lombardi was the head coach and general manager of the Green Bay Packers. When he joined the Packers, they were on a losing streak so bad that they'd only won one game the entire previous season. He led them to five championships in nine seasons and two Super Bowl victories. The Super Bowl trophy was named after him.

Lombardi knew all about the power of love. He loved his players and worked hard to do right by them, even if they didn't like him for it in the moment. He once said, "They may not love you at the time, but they will later." I wonder if that's what my dad thought when he gave me that spanking in the milking shed...?

Footballers have a reputation for being big, bad boys, and Lombardi's players were no exception. After joining the franchise in 1959, he brought in many new players, all of them huge. They were alphas. They were fast. They could take hits and get right back into it.

In the tough world of football, amidst all this masculinity, Lombardi focused on love. He fiercely insisted all players be treated equal, regardless of their race or sexuality. In the 60s, that wasn't common. He told businesses they'd be blacklisted if they discriminated against anyone on his team. He said he did not have black players or white players... he only had green players—the green of Green Bay Packers.

Being Human

Lombardi's attitude brought out the best in his players because, although we often revere footballers as superheroes, they are, in fact, human. All humans have one thing in common: we want to love and be loved.

This isn't news to you. We're comfortable with this idea in the wider world. We saw this when we talked about parenting. Many of us go to work in the first place because we have a family at home whom we love and want to provide for. Outside of work, we can talk about love in all forms. We love cars. We love nature. We love our military. We love watching Notre Dame and the 49ers win.

However, once we walk in the office door, no one talks about love (unless it's around the water cooler, analyzing last night's game). In business meetings, we rarely hear that word. Love is an issue, though, even if we don't say it out loud. Most leaders want their employees to love them, love the job, or — at the very least — love exceeding their goals.

If you want those things for your employees, then you, as their leader, must also be their parent. As my dad did for me, as Lombardi did for his players, that means showing love by holding your employees accountable.

The Parent, Not the Friend

We're not talking here about pampering your employees or trying to be their best friend. Leaders are parents, giving out chores, putting the kids before themselves, and holding them accountable to guide them to success.

When you look at parents treating their children as friends, you see that nobody is in charge. In friendships, all parties are treated equally with no one having authority over the other. Research published in *Parenting Science* by Gwen Dewar, Ph.D, shows that, "The authoritative parenting style is an approach to child-rearing that combines warmth, sensitivity, and the setting of limits. Parents use positive reinforcement and reasoning to guide children." This is exactly what it means to be a leader for your team.

Love and Commitment

Love is also about commitment. No matter how much you love your partner, it takes dedication to stay together after 15 years of him leaving the toilet seat up. In romantic relationships, these ideas are so intertwined that we don't give them much thought. When we look at love in other locations, though, commitment comes along for the ride.

As I write, a new football season just kicked off. I already know, no matter how my team does, I'll stay with them. I'm in it for good. When you love your car, you commit to keeping her clean, getting the oil changed, and quickly fixing anything that may dent her.

In the mattress stores, we used love to help the guest find their perfect mattress. When a guest had a hard time deciding which mattress they wanted, we would ask, "Out of all the mattresses you've tried, which one do you love the most?" This quickly helped the guest commit to a purchase. When they realized they loved that memory foam mattress, they got excited to pull out their credit card, make the investment, and get back to sweet dreams once again. It reflected on our bottom line; using that one question helped improve our closing rates. Our feedback and reviews improved because treating our customers as guests and showing them the love made them feel cared for.

If you want to see an improvement at work, you need to commit to it, which means enacting love into it.

This is Uncomfortable

If all this talk of love makes you squirm, if you want to slam this book shut and run away, wait just a moment and know your reaction is normal. Many leaders think it's weak to focus on love and hearts and all this soft stuff. It can be tough, especially if you see yourself as a strong leader. I've worked with all sorts of leaders, including harsh, rude men and women who wouldn't show their feelings. When I was being Hernazi, I was a bit like that. I refused to be vulnerable.

As soon as I let down my guard a little, when I started being more vulnerable, people came out to support me. When I admitted I didn't have all the answers, my team became more engaged. They got on board. They committed to the company and me. When my employees knew I loved them, they were willing to walk through walls for me. Moreover, I knew they wouldn't let me down. Don't you want that?

What is Workplace Love?

When I loved my team, it meant I cared about those individuals. I wanted to see them improve, progress, and have a long relationship with the company—or whatever workplace was best for them. I wanted them to succeed.

They embraced that sentiment and returned it. Just like looking in the mirror, what you see is what you get. So if you're rude, a pain in the butt, a real Hernazi, you'll get that same behavior back from your employees. If you show love in simple ways, by knowing exactly how they like their coffee, checking in on them when they or their family member is sick, by praising a job well done, you'll see those positive emotions reflected back to you.

They Must Know

It's vital to embrace love and accountability at work, but you also need to let your employees know they are loved. We often assume people know how we feel, but no one is a mind-reader.

Growing up, I don't think I ever told my parents I love them. I know what you're thinking... that's horrible. However, I don't remember my dad ever saying it to me, either. We did love each other. We just didn't say it. Then, in my thirties, I had a wake-up call. A colleague died unexpectedly. He was a young guy, and it came as a shock. I realized you never know when Father Time will show up for any of us, so we need to treat every interaction like it might be the last.

I started telling my parents I love them at the end of phone calls. It was awkward at first, but they said it back, and that felt magical. I'm so thankful I reached out of my comfort zone and started saying, "I love you." It felt like a quick win. We immediately had a stronger relationship. Soon, I started saying it when I left their house, too.

Last night, when I put my kids to bed, I told them I love them. I said that I believe in them and they mean everything to me. I won't wait for that magical experience, as I did with my parents, so I hold myself accountable to telling my children how I feel. Multiple times a day, I let them know they mean everything to me.

Can you tell people you love them, or do you find it a challenge, as I did with my parents? I'm not talking about your spouse or children here. I mean people slightly more removed: parents you haven't lived with for decades, teachers who made a lasting impression on you, colleagues or mentors who changed the course of your life.

If you have someone who means the world to you, tell them. Don't procrastinate any longer. Don't read any more of this book! Put it down, give them a call, or write them a message. I promise it will feel extremely magical for you and them. You will make their day.

It's sometimes hard to praise, compliment, or thank people. I've worked with some individuals who feel awkward, and they turn into a comedian. They make it funny or add a smart-ass contradiction to what would otherwise have been a touching comment. This is a natural tendency for many people, but it makes the whole thing sloppy. Try to make your message heartfelt. Look them in the eyes and be sincere.

If you're not used to talking like this, it's a huge step to reach out and tell that first person you love them. However, if you can't do it for someone you love, you're going to have a tough time talking to employees about how you feel. So get uncomfortable and practice showing your feelings. Here are some simple examples of using the term "love" in your communications:

"I love how you helped that customer."

"I love that you turned in this assignment way ahead of schedule."

"I love how proactive you are at preventing problems."

"I love your commitment to our team."

A New Approach

If you're still hesitant, take a moment to consider why your previous efforts to fix workplace problems haven't succeeded.

Now, think about how Lombardi's players spoke of him, years after leaving the team. Bart Starr, Packers quarterback from 1956 to 1971, recalls what Lombardi said at his first team meeting: "Gentlemen, we're going to relentlessly chase perfection." Perfection, Lombardi explained, was not actually attainable. But in the process of chasing perfection, "we will catch excellence."

Maybe it's time for a new approach, one that's rooted in love.

♥ Take Action

1. Outside of work, who has had a significant influence on your life? Think about teachers, mentors, leaders, coaches, family members, and friends.

2. List out the things they did to hold you accountable that helped you become who you are today.

3. Tell them you love them. Pick up the phone or write them a letter, and let them know what they've meant you to.

   For example: Hello [name], I've been wanting to tell you something for years. You were a big influence in my life, and I love the way you... [fill in the blank on what they did and mean to you].

[4]

THE 3PS

"The best way to predict your future is to create it."

—Abraham Lincoln, 16th president of the United States of America.

Before exploring accountability, I knew I needed a new approach to get the best from my employees. Over the years, I had them all; they ranged from 16-year-old kids wanting to earn enough to buy video games (or whatever it is kids want these days), to high-performing executives on a determined path to career success.

My reading and research suggested accountability was key, but it felt like a vague concept. As I learned from others and tried different strategies, I found it helpful to break accountability down and look at its components in more concrete terms.

I discovered there are three types of accountability: personal, positive, and performance. I tried, tested, and figured out the practical elements of those components, and this became the basis of the 3Ps program.

Balance in the Workplace

In the 1950s, people would've called me crazy for proposing a strategy that insists on being personal and positive. They'd have thrown me out of the boardroom for talking about love.

These days, thankfully, things have changed. More leaders are listening to their employees. There's research that supports these techniques I've seen work in the real world. We have a larger percentage of women in the workplace, bringing vital perspective and balance. There are fewer obstacles for minorities.

We've got a long way to go in balancing our businesses. It's a rough road, and there's much more we can do. However, the improvements we've seen so far have created more humane workplaces which are more successful by every metric.

The 3Ps program is all about balance. It's accountability that's fair and balanced for every member of the team, including you, the leader. We balance clear expectations and firm rules with generous praise and rewards.

Here's what it looks like...

P1: Personal Accountability

Personal accountability is the most important and challenging aspect of this program. It's important because, although it may not always feel like it, your employees want to follow you. They probably don't say it aloud, but they want to do what you do.

Just as a toddler will mimic your actions as you eat with a fork, stack blocks, and speak (particularly horrifying when your child copies you dropping that four-letter word), employees will copy you too.

That's not to say they're childish. It just shows that mimicry is part of human nature. It's how we all grew up to become functioning (or semi-functioning) adults, and it's how we continue to grow. Sometimes it's conscious. Often, it's not.

When I look at my own life, I can identify habits I've picked up from those around me. I embrace challenges, confident I can overcome them, after watching my parents overcome challenges in their lives. From Dale, the founder of Sleep Train, I learned to surround myself with people better and smarter than me, and find success by making them successful. My brother-in-law, Frank, taught me to always do what's convenient for the customer, and not what's convenient for me. His lesson became a habit I now use with both internal and external customers.

These are copied behaviors, and they're usually passed down from a more senior person to their junior; from parent to child, from the church minister to their congregation, teacher to student, and business leader to employee.

Because our employees copy us, we need to hold ourselves accountable before we can do the same for them. We need to make ourselves better, so we can lead by example. This is difficult, as it requires self-awareness. That doesn't come naturally to most of us, but it is essential.

For years, I've been friends with Robert Lorber, Ph.D., who co-authored *Putting The One Minute Manager to Work*, part of the enormously successful *One Minute Manager* book series and leadership training program. Robert is also professor who teaches leadership at UC Davis' Graduate School of Management. He told me someone can only take action when they have some self-awareness. A person must understand themselves before they can take action and change.

As we look at personal accountability, we'll develop that awareness. We'll be hard and honest with ourselves. We'll discover how to lead ourselves by changing how we think and act. This might not sound fun, but it can be. It starts with discussing how to be the hero at work, instead of the victim — and who doesn't want to be a hero? Then we'll talk about taking baby steps, being watched by your employees, and getting feedback on your own performance. If that sounds scary, don't worry. We'll cover all your concerns in chapter six.

P2: Positive Accountability

Then we'll move on to positive accountability. Positivity might sound like a "soft" subject, but it's essential to improving your bottom line and getting the results you want. Positivity is how good managers become great leaders. It's what led to my staff presenting me with a Best Leader Award. It's also more enjoyable than always being a negative nelly. Research tells us negativity is contagious and can have a detrimental effect on the workplace. Positivity is also contagious, and it's easy to create through your company's language.

When you get a company-wide email, and the subject line says, "Changes to health insurance," you start to freak out before you've even opened the attachment. Are they cutting support for my spouse? I bet they dropped dental coverage. My kid needs braces! Then you get a call, or a meeting reminder pops up, and you don't get a chance to read that email.

You spend all day with a stress headache before finally getting a chance to open the document. That's when you discover you're getting an extra teeth cleaning every year. By this time, you've already felt the stress and damage of negative language. When that email subject straight-up says, "Improvements to your health insurance," or "Extra teeth cleaning!" you don't freak out. Improvements are good. Thanks, company. You might not have time to read the attachment, but you go off to your meeting in a great frame of mind, able to give your best without distractions.

Positivity isn't just about language, though. As the old adage goes, actions speak louder than words, and we must take action to create positive experiences at work. There are so many ways to take positive steps and create excellent outcomes at work. We'll cover dozens of examples, so you can choose ideas that fit with your style and personality.

Of course, we all know it's not easy to be upbeat when your sales figures are in the tank, your staff insist on showing up late, and your boss is always on your back. We never want to sugar-coat a lousy situation, either. That's why we'll cover concrete action steps to make your workplace a more positive environment no matter the challenges you're facing, so you can reduce turnover, increase profitability, and actually enjoy your hours at work.

P3: Performance Accountability

The third P is performance accountability. This is more aligned with most people's understanding of accountability, you know, when you think of hauling someone up for their actions, discipline, or performance reviews. However, with our approach, you'll become a coach to your employees, helping them win at work and in life. Their success becomes your win and ultimately improves the organization.

The greatest coaches of all time teach us valuable lessons about improving performance to get those wins, and we'll look at their techniques. We'll also learn from the kid who pushed a shopping cart into my ankles at Home Depot. We'll review practical steps to improve onboarding new hires, leading your existing team, and handling an employee who does something unforgivable, so you're ready to handle any situation.

One, Then Two, Then Three

As you read the above descriptions of the 3Ps, one of them may have appealed to you more than the others. You might be drawn to a specific part of the program based on your personality, previous experiences—good and bad, and the unique challenges you're facing at work. Stop! It is essential you don't skip to that section. You must follow the 3Ps in order, P1, P2, then P3 so that you can benefit from these steps.

This is important, so I'll repeat: You have to follow the 3Ps program in order. It just doesn't work otherwise. If you jump around or choose to start in a different place, you won't create the foundation that's required for the latter techniques to work. You might be tempted to forge ahead with performance accountability because that's the category in which you see most of your current challenges. Your team isn't performing to the standards you expect, and you want to change that as soon as possible. I get it, and I understand you don't have all the time in the world to turn things around. If you try to jump straight in, though, without building a strong foundation with your own accountability and a positive environment, focusing on performance will make you a Hernazi. You'll come across as an overly strict, unfair dictator, and no one will want to work for you, let alone give you their best. That's exactly what happened to me, and it's how I earned that nickname. I don't want you to suffer the same.

If you follow performance accountability with positivity or jump straight there without the personal stuff first, people will think you're being fake. They'll assume you're acting all upbeat because you feel bad for holding them accountable. You won't seem genuine, even if you are, even if all your motivations are right. No one follows a leader who looks like a fake.

The Natural Flow of Things

Effective leadership starts with leading yourself. You become a better person, and then you can have a positive impact on those around you. You start seeing small wins, and they quickly snowball into massive success.

If you do P1: Personal Accountability and P2: Positive Accountability right, as you'll learn to in this book, P3: Performance Accountability will largely take care of itself. The things that feel difficult—coaxing better performance from your team members, stamping out destructive behavior, disciplining, hiring, and firing—will all happen with less effort or awkwardness.

That doesn't mean it's easy; there's a lot of work that has to happen on the front end to get you there. However, once you've covered that ground, you'll be so much more successful, in work and life, and it will flow naturally.

How to Use this Book

The rest of this book is divided into four sections. There's one section for each of the accountabilities:

personal, positive, and performance. In the final part, the conclusion, we talk about ways you, your employees, and your organization can become even greater. We discuss being accountable in the wider world, and I give you a glimpse into something particularly close to my heart.

Each section is further divided into chapters, each of which ends with questions and action items, just as you've already seen. Some of these will be an easy opportunity to drill the lessons into your head, and others will feel impossibly challenging. Take care to complete them all, because this time is an investment in you. Answering the questions and taking action is what will get you results. As Abraham Lincoln said at that beginning of this chapter, it's time for you to create your future.

♥ Take Action

1.   What are the 3P's of Accountability:

      P1:_____

      P2:_____

      P3:_____

2.   Why is it essential to progress through the 3Ps in order?

3.   Write a summary of each type of accountability, as if you were teaching them to a new leader in your workplace.

P1: Personal Accountability

Most Important Person

[5]

BE THE SUPERHERO

"The principle of competing is against yourself. It's about self-improvement, and being better than you were the day before."

—Steve Young, former NFL player and MVP of Super Bowl XXIX.

A couple of chapters ago, we talked about accountability being tied to love and looked at the incredible example set by football coach Vince Lombardi. Now, as we jump into the first of the 3Ps: Personal Accountability, I want to tell you the story of another football legend.

Steve Young was a quarterback who played 15 seasons in the NFL. He was named Most Valuable Player (MVP) twice and was MVP of Super Bowl XXIX. He's in both the College Football and Pro Football Halls of Fame. He knew all about the first facet of personal accountability: being the hero.

Despite all the highlights, Young threw 202 interceptions in his career. That's one heck of a lot of times that he threw the ball and the other team caught it. Every time it happened, his team would glare at him. Steve could've given many reasons why his throw was intercepted. He could've said the receiver didn't run their route, or the sun was in his eyes, or the offensive lineman didn't block well.

If he had, we can guess how the team would've reacted. They would've been mad at him. They would have sat down on the sidelines in disgust, and complained behind his back in the locker room.

But Young never said those things. Instead, he'd make sure everyone had water, bring them all together in a huddle on the sideline, and take the hit. He'd admit he messed up. He'd talk about his mistake. Then the team was freed from wasting energy on the interception. They'd talk it over, get out on the field, and get back to winning.

Time and time again—202 times in fact—Young took the hit so his team could move forward and be successful. That attitude helped make him a football legend and a great leader.

Will You Take the Hit?

You purchased this book, so I can confidently guess that things are challenging for you at work right now. At least, they're not as great as they could be. As my old college soccer coach would say, "there's room for improvement."

When things aren't going right at work, you have to decide if you will take the hit. Sure, there may be legit reasons why you're facing particular challenges. Some may be your fault; maybe you misjudged an action. Some might not; perhaps your teammate slacked off.

But if you want your team to win, you, the leader, have to take the hit. It's part of the job. Just as a quarterback must take responsibility for his throws, you must take responsibility for your team.

So, will you take the hit?

Now is the time to decide. Not tomorrow, when you're back at your desk or the job site. Not in your next meeting or performance review. Now.

As that wise, old transformer, Optimus Prime, said in Transformers: Age of Extinction, "Often, the most important moments in life come to this exact moment. What are you going to do?"

Choosing to take the hit is important. As we move through the book, you'll see it's the foundation for all your future success. I'll give you a moment to make your decision...

The Language of Losers

If you decided to take the hit, congratulations! That's a big deal. You're on the way to real change. You see, when you choose to take the hit, you stop making excuses. Excuses are the language of losers. The idea was drilled into me when I was nine-years-old, playing in my first ever soccer season.

Growing up, I used to play with anything that was round. I covered balls of paper with duct tape and lobbed them around the yard, kicked rocks, oranges, and balled-up socks. We couldn't afford a real soccer ball, but I made do with what we had. Mom put me in soccer to stop me ruining my socks, balling them up to kick them in the dirt.

As we lived in Jerome, Idaho, we'd get some bad weather toward the end of soccer season. In one of my first playoff games with the team, it snowed. It wasn't that fun, fluffy stuff; it was cold, wet, heavy snowflakes driving down onto the slippery pitch.

At half-time, we were losing 3-0. Our coach wasn't happy. He gathered us around and asked, "What's going on? You're getting your butts kicked out there." Us kids looked at each other and didn't say a word. He asked again, "What is it? Why are you playing so timid? You're better than this."

After a long moment, I decided I'd tell him. "We don't play well when it's snowing. The field sucks. And it's cold." Coach looked at me with disgust and said, "Are you kidding me? You're playing in the same weather, on the same field, as the other team. No more excuses."

It was brilliant. That one statement shut down all our excuses. We went out there and won the game. I don't remember the end score, but I do remember how empowered we felt in that second half.

After that, we actually wanted to play in bad weather. We knew the sleet and snow would get to the other teams, but we wouldn't let it stop us. Instead of whining about the cold, we focused on what we could control on the field. We went on to have a fantastic winning streak.

Are you Making Excuses?

Have you been making excuses in your game? Whatever you're working on; leading your team, reducing turnover, increasing sales, being a better partner or parent, have you made excuses for not performing your best?

It's human nature to look for someone or something else to blame. There's snow coming down on the pitch. Your predecessor at work hired all these idiots. Your boss has completely unrealistic expectations. Your kids just aren't interested.

No one is perfect. We are humans. We make mistakes. We make excuses.

But excuses are part of a victim mentality, which is the opposite of Steve Young's approach. Victim mentality is when we don't think about solutions but dwell on what went wrong, and whose fault it was, and all the reasons we're not to blame.

Of course, there's a time and place for considering what went sideways in a situation, or who should take the fall. But with a hero mentality, we ditch the excuses and focus on solutions first. With a victim mentality, we wallow in how unfair it all is and how powerless we are.

The Hero on the Hudson River

It would've been easy for Pilot Chesley Sullenberger, known to his friends—and later the world—as Sully, to take a victim mentality. On January 15, 2009, he was literally powerless as he flew a damaged Airbus A320 over New York. The story of what Sully did that day spread worldwide. Here's what happened...

That cold, January afternoon, he was captain of US Airways flight 1549, scheduled to fly from New York to North Carolina. With copilot Jeffrey Skiles, he took off from LaGuardia Airport with 155 souls on board. Initially, everything was normal. Sully had been flying for over 40 years and clocked up almost 20,000 hours of flight time. He knew what to expect from takeoff, and all was as expected.

But just two minutes in, disaster struck. Or, more precisely, geese struck. A large flock of Canada geese hit the plane, killing both engines. The plane had no power, and they were gliding just above the New York skyline.

Sully had to make a decision. He knew, from instinct, education, and experience, they wouldn't make it back to the airport. They didn't have enough altitude to glide that far. Within seconds, he assessed the situation and made the call: He would crash land in the Hudson River. He alerted the flight attendants and, with Skiles's help, prepared the plane for impact.

Emergency water landings are notoriously dangerous and rarely successful. But Sully brought that plane down in the middle of the ice-cold river and saw all 155 passengers safely evacuated. He was last to leave the sinking plane. There were no fatalities. It's since been called, "the most successful ditching in history."

We can take a lot of inspiration from Sully's heroic actions to bring that plane down safely in unbelievably difficult circumstances. His dedication to the job, expertise, and character are all awe-inspiring. But I want to focus on his mindset in the minutes between the engine failure and hitting the water.

Sully and Skiles have since described those 190 seconds. They talked about the eerie silence in the cockpit, with no familiar hum of engines behind them. They told how they worked quickly through emergency checklists, changing settings and flight paths, and talking to air traffic control. Sully described, "the worst sickening, pit-of-your-stomach, falling-through-the-floor feeling" right before impact.

There are a few things notably missing from their testimony. Not once did they mention panic, getting mad, or asking why. Of course, Sully could easily have panicked. He was in charge of that plane and responsible for the lives on board.

He could've become instantly furious with those dumb birds for flying right into them. I'm sure road rage occurs in the air just as it does on solid ground. Or he could've sat there in desperation and thought, If only.... If only the passengers had boarded faster... If only we'd departed a minute earlier this would not have happened.

He didn't waste time with that, though. It may not have been a conscious move, but when a crisis struck, he immediately shifted into a hero mentality. What can I do to save the day? How do I get us down safely?

Serious Stuff

Your life might not be as dramatic as the scene on the Hudson that day. Maybe you think you won't encounter life-threatening situations at work, as he did. You're wrong. Workplace safety is serious stuff.

This may be obvious if you work on dangerous job sites or with heavy equipment, for example. You have standard operating procedures and safety protocols to follow. You know what to do to prevent things going wrong, and have guidelines for when they go wrong anyway.

You might work in a more mundane environment, though. For you, the stapler might be the most dangerous equipment around. I know, from decades of working in "safe" environments, that you'll still encounter serious safety decisions. What about letting that employee drive home after too many drinks at the company party?

Life-saving safety decisions aside, your attitude can have a life-changing impact on your employees. It can be the trigger that helps them win, just as Steve Young so often did with his team.

If your natural instinct is to fall into a victim mindset, you should know this is a normal part of being human. However, it's something you must address if you want to be a great leader.

It's not easy to ditch the victim mentality, particularly if it's become a habit for you. It also hard when horrible things happen to us. That's life. There will be people who let us down, someone who cuts us off, accidents that occur, bills that don't get paid, and the deaths of special people in our lives.

When these horrible things happen, I take inspiration from Garrett Matthias...

Garrett and the Asgardian Burial

Garrett was just five years old when he found out he was dying. He had a rare form of cancer called alveolar fusion negative rhabdomyosarcoma. A five-year-old shouldn't even know what it means to die, but Garrett understood acutely. In the pediatric cancer ward, he'd seen many of his playmates pass away.

As his cancer spread and treatment failed, he refused to sit in a victim mentality, feeling sorry for himself. He ditched the excuses—I'm too sick, it's too hard—and decided to take control of how he'd be remembered once he was gone.

He wrote his own obituary, which ended, "See ya later, suckas!" and planned the most fun funeral he could imagine. He asked his parents for five bouncy houses, one for each year of his life. He requested an Asgardian burial, like in the movie Thor: An archer would shoot a fiery arrow at his ashes as they floated on a lake near his home. He asked for Batman to attend and eat snow cones.

His parents fulfilled his wishes. For his celebration of life, they hired actors to dress as Batman, Wonder Woman, and Spiderman. Garrett's daycare classmates attended wearing Batman t-shirts they embossed with the letter G. Friends and family ran around munching on snow cones, with their faces painted. They even found an archer for the Asgardian burial.

Remembering Garrett, his grandfather, Fred Krueger, said even after the cancer progressed, Garrett's gracious nature did not change. "He was laying there, and he was paralyzed, and I was sitting in a crappy, old chair, and he said, 'Grandpa, come over here and sit on the recliner. It will be more comfortable for you.' Now, a five-year-old doing that is almost unheard of."

Garrett will be remembered for that gracious nature. I didn't know him personally, but I know he had that hero mentality. He found ways for Grandpa to be more comfortable even while he himself was suffering.

Of course, I hope none of us ever suffer as Garrett did. I also hope we can learn from him to embody that hero attitude. Or, as Garrett would more likely say, superhero attitude.

♥ Take Action

1. What excuses have you been making at work?

2. How can you take the hit and be a hero for your team?

3. At work, pay close attention to how many excuses you hear from others around you. Once you become more aware of these excuses, you'll find it difficult to ever utter one again.

[6]

YOUR FRIENDS: ME, MYSELF, AND I

"I am still learning."

—Michelangelo, famed Italian sculptor and painter, at age 87.

Does accountability require a carrot or a stick? That's a common question when considering how to motivate employees to improve their performance. Since I spent several chapters going on about love and heroes, you may think I'm all about the carrots.

But it's neither. Carrots... sticks... they have their place. But employee motivation is all about you.

As a leadership consultant, I go into businesses and sit down with their executive teams to discuss their challenges, and how we can maximize the company's potential by winning the hearts and minds of their employees.

My first meeting with a leadership team is usually in a boardroom, all sat around a table, the executives fidgeting uncomfortably because I won't let them check email on their phones while we talk. As we get chatting, they realize I'm not there to criticize but to help them get the results they desperately want.

They relax, and I ask them, "Who is the most important person in the world to you?" The answers are what you'd expect. It's usually, My mom, my wife, my husband, my kids. Then, I ask again. They're intelligent folks, so they know I'm fishing for a different answer. After a pause, they figure it out.

The most important person in the world is themselves.

You First

Think of when the flight attendant says to put your own oxygen mask on first. You can't get your son out of the plane if you're passed out on the seat beside him because you were too busy fixing his mask to get yourself any air.

Next, I ask the team, "What do you control about yourself?" The answer is everything. This isn't rocket science, but it gives those busy, stressed-out executives a moment to reflect, and remember that they control themselves.

This is a good reminder for all of us. It's a reality check that reveals it's not everyone else's fault when you're not getting the results you want. You can't control the world, but you can take charge of your own actions.

Take a moment to consider how this sits with you. Do you find it empowering? Does it overwhelm you? Maybe there's a bit of both going on. These ideas may even bring forth some guilt when you realize you could've taken control of your crummy work situation, but didn't.

It's okay. Don't let that guilt get to you. You picked up this book because you want to do better. Life is one long learning process. Michelangelo was 87 when he said, "I am still learning." This was the man who painted the Sistine Chapel in his mid-30s!

It sounds counter-intuitive, but when you learn to look after yourself first, you will do better—for you and everyone around you. We'll work on this together, as it's not an easy idea to fulfill.

When you're in that plane and see your child sitting there, knowing oxygen levels are plummeting, instinct makes you reach for their mask first. In the cold light of day, though, when we can see the situation objectively, we know we need to attend to ourselves before them. It's a hard move, but undoubtedly the right one.

In the context of improving your performance as a leader, the right move requires you to check yourself. To look after yourself first, you must check that you are accountable. Check your behavior at work, social events, and even on the internet aligns with your goals for work and life.

In the Partners in Leadership Workplace Accountability Survey, 8 out of 10 employees said their leader's behavior was the single most important accountability influence in their organization.

The burden is on you, but don't let it be overwhelming. When you understand the impact certain behaviors have on your organization, you can choose how to control them. That's empowering.

Checking Yourself Online

Social media is a funny thing. It's a void where people's behavior can spiral. I'm sure you can recall examples of leaders making shockingly inappropriate comments online. It can feel all too common with political figures and famous CEOs, but we also see this on a smaller scale.

There was the real estate agent who shared a photo of her client. He was standing next to an old, beat-up car, and looked pretty beat-up himself. She added the caption; Can you believe I got this person a home? She was making fun of her client. I guess she thought he'd never see it, and maybe he didn't. But others did, and I'll bet they'll think twice before using her as their realtor.

On some of my friends' Facebook walls, I see people talking badly about others. I see drunk posts and pictures of half-naked people. And these are from good people and great friends!

Even posts that aren't intended to be nasty can have a negative impact. Commenting on public affairs–Did you see so-and-so on TV last night? Can you believe that political candidate?—can be a slippery slope to stereotyping. It's easy to inadvertently make assumptions about others, and other people can stereotype you based on one isolated comment.

If you are a leader, you are in the public eye. This probably isn't on the same scale as political leaders or celebrities, but even so, you are under the watch of those who work for or are influenced by you. This is especially true if you are leading a team that is younger than you.

They really are watching. I'm sure you know your employees are on social media. That's no surprise. But you may be interested to hear how curious they are about you. They want to know details of your life, whether they admit it openly or not.

Don't Run, Be Human

Knowing you face scrutiny and seeing the pitfalls, you may be tempted to run a million miles from social media. That was me. For a long time, I was a resistor. I was not the social media guy.

Then, I started to understand the risks of refusing to engage and the benefits of being visible. You see, it's not normal to shut down, not letting your employees know anything about you. If you're secretive about your life, you become distant and invulnerable.

But when you let employees see what makes you human—how much you love your chocolate lab, eating game day nachos with friends, cuddling your kids, getting hopped-up on Halloween candy—it bridges the gap between you and them. When done with respect, that transparency always improves relationships.

Doing this well requires you accept social media for what it is. It should not be an outlet for spewing political views and religious rants. Instead, it's a platform to show you are a real person and to demonstrate the same attitudes you are trying to foster at work.

It's tricky because social media is personal, and traditionally, society has bundled personal and private together. But in the online world, this doesn't apply. You can use social media to successfully support you as a leader if you remember that sharing on a personal level builds relationships, but sharing does not stay private.

There must be a balance between personal and private. You shouldn't over-indulge by posting when drunk or sharing unfiltered opinions about clients. You can't be nonexistent, either. It sounds challenging to get this balance right, but it just requires some caution.

Share as much as you're comfortable with. If you're in doubt about something, don't press send. If your funny comment on a friend's video has the potential to hurt, it's not worth a few likes.

Proceed with caution, show you're human, and social media will improve your image and employee relationships.

One Step at a Time

Being cautious doesn't mean you must become a complete killjoy online or in "real" life. You just have to check your behaviors one at a time, to ensure they'll help you reach your goals.

If your goal is to lose 10 pounds, you start by switching a chocolate bar for a bowl of fruit. You make one good decision, followed by another. You take baby steps to achieve success. That's what we'll do here.

After checking your online behavior, the next baby step is to consider how you currently communicate with your team. Then, we'll review the ideal methods of communication, and how they will help you reach your workplace goals. Many times we look at communication about how we communicate, when in reality should focus on how we make others feel.

How Do You Communicate?

Communication is one of the biggest challenges in business and relationships. We've all seen disasters happen when people fail to communicate properly. Marriages fall apart. Customer service standards drop. You show up promptly at 7pm for a movie that started at 6pm.

I've seen organizations vow to combat this issue by over communicating. They promise they'll send plenty of company-wide messages and hold weekly town hall meetings. They commit to talking about everything. This sounds great but seldom works. Instead of reaching for the unrealistic (and frankly, annoying) goal of over communicating, ask how you can improve your current communication methods.

When I work with new clients, they're often leaders who are frustrated with their employees. "The staff don't read their emails," they say. "They won't prepare for meetings. They don't tell me when they have problems."

By now, you probably expect me to say that I turn their attention from the team back to themselves. You're right. You're so smart. Instead of dwelling on what the team does wrong, we dig into how the leader communicates out to that team. The common denominator is them.

I ask the leader to rank their methods of communication by frequency. Do they have big team meetings more than one-on-one sessions? If they work on the road, are they more likely to jump on a video call or send a text message?

Whatever the work setup, email always comes out high on the list. Often, text messages are second, followed by group meetings. Phone calls and one-on-one meetings fall somewhere near the bottom. Does this sound familiar?

As email ranks so far ahead of other methods of communication for almost every person, it's a great place to take some baby steps. We'll cover the various methods of communication throughout the book, but email is so common and so troublesome, we have to address it now.

Email Guidelines Will Rescue You

Email done right is great. However, most of the time it's done wrong and becomes easily the worst form of communication. Technology is a great tool when we are balanced. It's too easy to send a message to a bunch of people, and hope they read and understood it. Plus, you can't take an email back once it's gone.

This makes it dangerous to send emails when you're fired up. Go ahead and write that message slamming your team member for showing up late, but don't send it. Keep it in your drafts folder. Don't ever send that email. If you're in doubt, delete it. After waiting 24 hours, use that email as a template for a real conversation, in person or on the phone, with the team member in question.

Aside from ensuring your emails aren't angry, you should make them friendly... hamster friendly. When I worked at Sleep Train, we took the whole company through the principles outlined in the book The Hamster Revolution: How to Manage Your Email Before It Manages You. Authors Mike Song, Vicki Halsey, and Tim Burress share many great guidelines for successful emails. One that stuck with us was to use a simple ABC structure.

Use ABC Emails

Start your email with A: the ACTION you want the recipient to take. Then move on to B: any relevant BACKGROUND information, in bullet point format. Finish with C: the CLOSE, which keeps emails short and well-structured, less than 100 words is ideal. Here's what it looks like in action:

Hi Liz,

Action: By next Thursday, please send me the budget forecast for the fourth quarter, assuming a 6 percent increase in advertising spend.

Background:
- Veterans holiday lands on a Thursday this year.
- Be sure to take into account the heavy political advertising starting in September and running through to election day.
- For more details, see our last Friday's meeting notes in our team folder.

Close:

I loved the feedback you provided at our meeting. You have become a great mentor for the team.

Many thanks,

Hernani Alves

This simple structure streamlined our emails and removed a lot of frustration. There are many ways to improve email communication. Entire books are dedicated to the subject (The Hamster Revolution is an excellent one). The point is to create email guidelines that will work for your company. Below are a few more guidelines we implemented, which might help you, too.

Limit Use of Reply-to-All

Reply-to-all is one of the biggest complaints amongst employees. When the sender sends this email, they assume everyone needs to know the information. Then, someone feels they need to respond, and so does the next person, and so on. I call this the email firing squad. It fills up your inbox with nonsense. Please challenge yourself, and ask, Do I really need to send this email to everyone or just to the people that need this information. If you do need to send your email to multiple people, you can add a note that stops the firing squad in its tracks: Please only reply to me, instead of replying to all. Your employees will love you for this.

Don't BCC

BCC stands for Blind Carbon Copy. With this function, you can copy someone on an email without letting the original recipient know. BCC shouldn't exist. It's a scapegoat. It's talking behind someone's back. If you need to share an email conversation, forward it to the new person with a note addressing them properly.

Make Your Response Expectations Clear

During a team meeting, I challenged our team to develop email guidelines everyone could follow that would support the business and maximize productivity. Here are the ones we came up with and used. My team and I loved them.

Successful Email Guidelines

1. Always write hamster friendly emails (using the ABC method) with deadlines.
2. Don't expect a response within 48 hours unless noted in the subject line.
3. Immediate response (same day) emails require a phone call.
4. If you're not available that day, you must use the out-of-office email function.
5. Action emergency emails are NOT allowed. You must call, instead.
6. During vacation, emails will not be checked.
7. When off duty and at home, emails will not be checked. If needed, call instead.
8. If you are CC'd on an email, you do not need to respond.

Your business model may require different standards, but determine what they are with your team, and ensure everyone knows them.

Only Check Emails Three Times a Day

Instead of checking email every ten minutes, as so many people do, check your inbox just three (or, if you can't resist, four) times a day. This will create valuable time for you and your employees to focus and get your work done. In a study at the University of British Columbia, researchers found when people were limited to checking their email just three times a day, their stress levels decreased significantly. It allows you to stay focused and be more productive on the task at hand. Do you reach the end of the day and wonder why you didn't get everything done that you'd wanted? Regularly checking your emails, is many times the culprit.

The Goal for Communication Methods

While these guidelines will improve your written communications with your team, ideally you should push email to the bottom of your rankings list. You want your most important conversations to happen one-on-one. Here's what your future rankings list should look like:

Best forms of communication, ranked by productivity

- One-on-one
- Video call
- Phone call
- Text message
- Email

That might seem like an unattainable goal, especially if your employees don't work near you. As you go through this book, you'll discover how to use other methods of communication to improve accountability and create a better workplace.

We'll talk about how to do one-on-one meetings (both the fun, "welcome to the team" type and the harder, "goodbye forever" ones), when video and phone calls are useful, and how to use text messages.

In the meantime, we have more to work on in P1: Personal Accountability. The next baby step is to recognize what others say when they watch you.

♥ Take Action

1. Do you look after yourself first, or will this be a new challenge? How do you feel about checking your behavior?

2. Look at your social media posts this past year. Which ones do you regret and what can you do better moving forward? If you're not on social media, choose a platform (such as Facebook, LinkedIn, or Instagram), set up an account, and start using it.

3. Working with your team, create and implement a short list of email guidelines for your workplace.

THEY ARE WATCHING YOU

"If you want to be a leader, the first person you have to lead is yourself."

—Mike Scioscia, Major League Baseball manager and former player.

My daughter was about eight years old when we put a soccer net up in our backyard. I told you how much I loved kicking a ball around as a kid, right? I was about her age when I really got into the beautiful game, so I'd decided it was time to teach Carmina how to score goals.

Our first backyard session was a lot of fun. We were passing back and forward and hitting goals on net (which, admittedly, wasn't too hard given there was no goalkeeper and we were about five yards away). But Carmina was a bit timid. I wanted her to kick harder.

"You kick like a girl!" I said, trying to motivate her.

"Dad," she said. "I am a girl. How do you want me to kick?" My point was lost. She had no idea what I meant, because she was innocent and uncorrupted, and had not yet been trained by the world to mistakenly think girls are the weaker sex.

The women in my life are essential and equal to me, and I'm well aware of their strength. But even I had accidentally made a chauvinistic comment. I was humbled.

"You're right. I want you to kick like a superhero," I said. Carmina understood, and she kicked the ball harder.

This small moment with my daughter taught me to watch my words. They have an impact. My daughter hears what I say and watches what I do. My words and behavior will carry weight as she forms her own views of the world.

Your employees are watching you. They are adults (unless your employing child labor, in which case you have bigger issues than accountability. We should talk.) Adults aren't as susceptible to subconscious messaging as an eight-year-old, but they do learn what is and is not acceptable from you. They also pay just as much attention to your off-the-cuff comments as Carmina did to mine.

I was barely aware of that throwaway comment. If she hadn't said anything, I'd never have remembered the words I used to try to motivate her. But Carmina was highly aware of what I said because children magnify their parents' behavior.

Employees notice—and remember—the things you say and do, too. It's not because they're childish; They're mature, intelligent adults who are paying attention to their leader so they can learn what's expected of them. But while scanning for those signals, they pick up other things, too. In their search for support, they magnify everything you do.

Common Habits

Carmina put a spotlight on my comment, "You kick like a girl." This is just one example of a bad language habit I picked up over my lifetime. It came from decades playing sports in communities who didn't consider how damaging that sentence can be.

Like me, you probably have some bad language habits you're not aware of, that others are uncomfortable with. We grow up influenced by society, and it's normal to pick up these habits without properly considering what they mean. We're going to talk about two common ones so you can see what they look like, then we'll review how to identify habits unique to you.

That's gay

Too many people say, "that's gay" when they really mean "that's stupid." Stupid and gay are not synonyms. To use them that way is discrimination. It implies gay people are stupid, which is not true.

If you've said this, I know you probably don't mean it that way. It was just a language habit you picked up somewhere. I bet you value your gay employees just as much as the straight ones.

You may not even know your employees' sexuality. It might not matter to you (and rightly so). But that phrase means something to your gay team member who hears you say a core part of their identity is dumb.

Husbands and wives

Another common bad language habit is how we talk about families. When I grew up, a family was a husband, a wife, and a handful of kids who looked like them. It was probably the same for you, right?

Today, family can mean many things. Thankfully, we've expanded our concept of what love looks like. Two dads or two moms is becoming more common. Single parents and step-parents are everywhere. We're seeing grandparents as guardians, adopted children, unmarried couples as committed as the married ones, and happy, blended families of all shapes.

Whatever your family looks like, it might be different for your employees. I know you're already aware of this, but does your team know you know? Do you talk about family in a way that shows their own set-up is respected?

Asking a new employee what his wife's name is might seem innocent. But if he's gay, divorced, single, or living with his long-term girlfriend, that simple question subtly suggests his living situation is not what's expected in your team.

You don't mean it that way. You probably don't care if he's been married for decades, or shares his bed with no one but his pet poodle. It doesn't matter. You're still sending a subconscious signal to your new employee that he doesn't belong because he's not the same.

You don't need to change everything to make that employee feel welcomed. It often only takes one word: In this situation, spouse instead of wife. Asking if he has a spouse, instead of assuming he does and that it must be a wife, can make all the difference to someone who is eager to be accepted. And isn't that all of us?

Identifying Your Bad Language Habits

You can now see what bad language habits look like. They're simple, subtle, and have a big impact on the listener. I could give dozens of more examples, but every leader is unique and will have their own habits that are magnified by their team. Thankfully, I have a top tip that will help you figure yours out.

Have you ever told a joke then realized no one is laughing quite as much as you? I have. Maybe it's because jokes about chickens who crossed the road are never funny. But there's a good chance the crickets are because the punchline offended someone.

Reflect on those moments. If you were laughing louder than your employees, they were probably only joining in because you're the boss. It sucks, but that's usually how it goes.

I was once brought in to help a leader deliver some distressing news to his employees. The company was laying off many of the staff. We didn't have much time to prepare, so we focused on the core content of his speech. We didn't talk about "connecting with the audience." This leader did want to connect and show empathy, which was fantastic. His heart was in the right place.

Unfortunately, he got uncomfortable delivering the layoff details and reached to humor to connect and soften the blow. The team stood before him, panicky despair written across their faces. Their minds were clearly racing ahead. How will I pay the mortgage next month? I spent our last savings on fixing the car. What will I tell the kids?

"Hey, I'm in this with you," the leader said. "I'm probably going to have to sell my lake house." Poor choice. It was supposed to be a joke, but everything about it was off.

In that case, it wasn't even that his employees laughed less than him. There was an awkward silence which made it loud and clear the joke was offensive.

Now, don't get me wrong. I like a good joke. I also enjoy really awful, cheesy jokes. If you have any, email them over. I'd love to hear them. Bonus points if they're appropriate to share with my kids.

But I don't make jokes in sensitive moments, for example, when someone's just been told they're losing their income. Those jokes tend to send the wrong message. Even avoiding that, I've still misjudged in other situations and had to eat my words. I've learned from experience.

Now, I repeat a joke in my mind a few times before saying it out loud. If I feel it could be taken out of context, I skip it. I keep things light and use caution. It's a good balance. While you look for this balance, remember your jokes are being watched with a critical eye, and the response will tell you when you slip up.

Coming Back from a Slip-Up

If your team isn't comfortable speaking up, you'll have to rely on your own introspection and observation skills to see when you've slipped up. But if you're lucky, your employees and colleagues will call you out.

There were times when my team called me out on bad language habits. Sometimes I was trying to be funny, and an employee would look up and say, "Hey Hernani, that's not cool." In those moments, I had to choose how to respond.

The worst possible response is an excuse. It was just a joke. Lighten up. I didn't mean it. That's victim mentality. Underneath that thought, you're really saying, "Poor me. I was just trying to tell a joke and now they're ganging up on me."

Hero mentality is stepping up and saying, "You're right. I'm sorry." It's taking the hit and accepting your words or actions were offensive—even if you didn't mean them to be. Hero mentality is apologizing. Sorry is a magic word. It removes the tension and lets you move on. Sorry is how you come back from a slip-up.

Being Watched Outside of Work

Your employees are watching you. This is true both when you're in and outside of work. When you're off the clock, you're still being scrutinized. We've already talked about them watching you on social media. Your team members will also notice how you conduct yourself at Friday night drinks, at the company Christmas party, and staff appreciation lunches. Any social event counts.

Jim, an employee of mine at Sleep Train, discovered this the hard way. I had always been a big fan of his. He got great results at work, was fun to be around, and was a genuinely good guy. He'd been considered several times for a promotion.

But he didn't get any of those opportunities. Why? We didn't believe he'd be respected as a leader. Everyone knew he could do the job but at company celebrations, he always... had more fun than everyone else. Fun isn't bad. Fun is fun. But time after time he drank too much. It seemed he was having a tough time with alcohol.

My heart went out to him. Addictions are horrible things to suffer through. The fact remained, though: Jim's behavior at social events insured he wouldn't be respected as a leader and was, therefore, a poor choice for promotion.

Water, Please

Early in my career, I was that guy. Thankfully not addicted, but drinking too much at company events, making poor decisions, and embarrassing myself. I saw it could hurt my prospects, so made a conscious decision to change my strategy. Now, I start with a real drink, then switch to soda water with lemon. People usually mistake it for a vodka soda, which keeps the peer pressure away.

Don't be afraid to drink water at a work event. When everyone is a bit tipsy, and you're still talking straight, you'll seem really smart. Staying sober doesn't just stop you jeopardizing your reputation. It enables you to look out for your employees, just like you'd be there for your family.

When you're thinking clearly, you can get your team member a cab home if they've had too much. You can spot the new girl standing alone in the corner, and draw her into the team's conversation. You can get to know your staff better, and show them some love. Most importantly, you'll remember your employees' guests names and the conversations you had that evening. For me, that's far more important than getting drunk.

You can't be the leader that celebrates too much. That might seem like the most depressing sentence in this book, but it's not. And no, that's not because the following chapters are packed with even more depressing stuff. It's because accepting this statement gives you power.

Remember what you wanted when you picked up this book? Think about the state of your workplace right now, and how much better it could be. Imagine if your team was performing at its best, you were hitting work goals out of the park, and enjoying being there each day.

Staying sober at work events will help you get there. You'll still have fun—I do—and you'll feel the satisfaction of knowing you're earning respect from your team. You'll be proud of your effort. This is a small act entirely within your control, and it can make a real difference in reaching your goals. That's exciting.

Let's Get Uncomfortable

Do you feel uncomfortable knowing your employees are watching you? Does it make you want to run away and hide in an off-the-grid mountain cabin, eating wild squirrels and drinking rainwater filtered through your sock? Yuck.

This can be uncomfortable. You're not alone if you feel that way. Considering your language habits, work conduct, and social behavior can be challenging. I encourage you to do so, though, because getting uncomfortable paves the way for great things to happen.

Tracy, the human resources executive I worked so closely with, ends her meetings with "let's get uncomfortable" sessions. She goes around the room and asks each team member, including herself, to describe a situation that week that made them uncomfortable. Together, they brainstorm ways to handle that situation if it comes up again. Everyone learns, improves, and discovers it's okay to be uncomfortable.

It's okay for you, too. Discomfort won't kill you. It'll just help you improve.

Don't Change; Improve

Did you notice what I said? You'll improve. The improvement requires some change, but when you focus on the word change, it gets harder. For most of us, that word carries a lot of negativity.

I once went to a group of salespeople and told them I was going to change their pay. It was getting better, but they still got very defensive with me. That was a tough meeting. With the next group, I told them I was going to improve their pay. What a different experience.

You might resent having to change. Maybe you hate having to hold yourself personally accountable before your team falls into step. But do you hate improving? Do you resent it when work gets exponentially better? No, I didn't think so. So don't change; just improve. Change = Improvements.

♥ Take Action

1. It's usually easier to spot other people's bad habits than our own. So, to get used to seeing this stuff, what poor language, jokes, and behaviors have you witnessed from others?

2. How did you respond and what would you do differently next time?

3. Have an uncomfortable conversation to find your bad language habits and behaviors. Ask three close people if they'll give you some honest feedback. When they say yes (because they will say yes), ask if there are any leadership behaviors you can improve on.

[8]

THE GIFT OF FEEDBACK

"We all need people who will give us feedback. That's how we improve."

—Bill Gates, founder of Microsoft and co-chair of the world's largest private charitable foundation.

If you completed the action items from the last chapter, you might have received some challenging feedback. It might've made you a bit defensive, coming up with excuses or justifying your decisions. Ignoring negative comments is another common tactic you may have resorted to. Or you might be feeling down on yourself, thinking, Thanks, Hernani. Now I feel lousy.

Maybe... you didn't do the action items. You didn't ask anyone for feedback on your language and behavior, because you knew you'd feel defensive, down on yourself, or guilty for ignoring the comments.

No one wants to feel like that. I didn't. In my Hernazi days, I couldn't accept feedback. I had a tough time. I was arrogant back then. I thought I was Mr. Perfect, and the negative comments were just everyone's way of trying to sabotage me. I was getting results and winning glory, which boosted my oversized ego, so I didn't think I needed anyone's input.

Then, my district manager cut me down to size. His name was Matt Jessell, and he was more than just my manager. He was the person who hired me at Sleep Train, and he'd become my mentor. I liked Matt. More importantly, I respected him.

"You're outstanding and one of the best salespeople we have. However, no one wants to work with you," he said. Ouch. That left a scar.

His feedback pushed me to take action, and I did exactly what you're doing right now. I read a book. I chose the business classic How to Win Friends and Influence People by Dale Carnegie, and Whale Done: The Power of Positive Relationships by Ken Blanchard.

Those books helped me realize I was imperfect and needed to improve. I didn't know it then, but I was developing my personal accountability. As Bill Gates says, people who give us feedback help us improve. That's what Matt did for me. Thanks, Matt!

Ugly Gifts

Matt also told me to see feedback as a gift. This is a great attitude to have. It really helps when you hear negative feedback. His comment that no one wanted to work with me? That was an ugly statement, but it was a gift, nevertheless.

It's like the ugly sweater you get from Great Aunt Muriel. You know she sent it with good intentions, but that doesn't mean you like the purple and green zig zag pattern or glittery golden baubles hanging off it.

But do you write to Aunt Muriel and ask why she sent such an ugly sweater? No. At least, I hope not. You are nice, and you say thank you. And who knows... you could find a use for that knitted mess. You could wear it to an ugly sweater party someday.

The same thing happens when you get a gift you already have. Two handmade sweaters with purple and green zig zags? Lucky you. But you won't be rude to the person who gives you the second sweater. You say thank you, then maybe re-gift it to another friend attending an ugly sweater party.

You won't like some feedback you get. It will be tough to hear. People will say things you don't believe, or already know. It's all a gift. You can choose to accept it and wear the sweater, put it in your closet and use it at a later date, or re-gift it to someone else—like I'm doing with this book, re-gifting feedback given to me.

Appreciating feedback as a gift will help you improve as a leader, so you can create a stronger, more productive team. It's also essential for the next step in personal accountability: a personal engagement survey.

What is a Personal Engagement Survey?

I start working with leaders when they've dug themselves a hole. They're sitting in the bottom of a deep, dirty well, still shoveling away because they don't know what else to do.

If you don't know how to improve things at work and feel like all your actions just sink you deeper into that hole, you need to get rid of the shovel. Then, you need people to hand you a ladder, because you won't get out of there alone. The only way out is with help from others.

We learned to throw away the shovel in chapter five when we discussed taking the hit and accepting responsibility for the challenges at work. We're going to use that tactic, then enlist other people to pass you the ladder. That's what the personal engagement survey does. It engages other people in your personal accountability process, so they can give you the gift of feedback, and you can finally climb out of the hole.

How to Conduct Your Personal Engagement Survey

Step 1. Set the stage

We'll keep this really simple. You'll need a room, and two flip charts. On one flip chart, write, Things I've done that you liked and want more of. On the other, write, Things I need to do less of.

Step 2. Gather your team and take the hit

Bring your team together, talk about the challenges you have at work, and say they stem from an accountability challenge. Take the hit and admit the situation is your responsibility. Admit you want to become a better leader for them, and describe how this activity will help you be personally accountable.

Step 3. Describe the activity

Your team is going to think about your actions in the last six months. You'll leave the room, and on one flip chart, they'll list things you've done that they liked and want to see more of. On the other, they'll list actions they want to see less of. Then, you'll use their feedback to create an action plan that will improve your leadership skills.

When your employees first hear this, they'll think, Uh oh. The room might get a bit tense. Saying negative things about the leader can be scary. But when they hear you're taking the hit and want their help to get out of the hole, they'll relax. That will lower their stress levels, and you can get on with a productive session.

Step 4. Leave the room

Leave the room for 30-minutes and let your team work together to form ideas without you. While you're waiting, do the exercise yourself. What has your team responded well to, that you could do more of in the future? What hasn't worked?

You might be tempted to skip this step and spend the time checking emails or organizing your fantasy football team. Don't. When you do the exercise yourself, you'll be able to compare your ideas to those of your team. You could discover something you thought was valuable doesn't matter to the group. Maybe you're patting yourself on the back for bringing doughnuts to team meetings, but they're trying to lose weight and want bananas instead. You won't know unless you get your ideas down before hearing theirs.

Step 5. Go back and listen

At the 30-minute mark, go back into the room. Sit down and ask the team to tell you more about each item listed on the Like and do more of flip chart. This is very important: All you need to say is, "Tell me more about X." Then, have them talk you through the Do less of list. These items will be more difficult to hear, but don't challenge them. You shouldn't explain, justify, or offer excuses. Commit to listening and trying to understand the key actions in the examples you're given. Remember: No excuses or you'll just dig a bigger hole.

Step 6. Filter and take action

Thank your employees for sharing with you, and let them know you value their feedback. Then, take time to sit with their comments and filter out anything that's not helpful.

Sometimes, employees use this opportunity to spout all their stories, and you get blamed for things that don't even pertain to you. This one time... at band camp.... Then there are mean comments from people whose mothers didn't hug them enough as children.

You can filter out those random comments, but if you keep getting the same feedback, you'd better start listening. Review what you've heard and look for common denominators. Find the recurring themes. Then decide what action you'll take so you can use this gift to improve.

What If Your Team Is Spread Out?

If you can't get your team in a room together, you can do this online. It's not ideal, though. If you have the opportunity, it's best to wait and get everyone together in person. Something magical happens when your employees look you in the eye, with no screen between you, and hear you say, "I need help." That will stir something in your team, and they will want to rally around you.

When that's not possible, video conferencing is the next best option. These things don't come across well in email, so steer clear of that approach. In a video conference scenario, you can take the hit and explain the exercise live on camera, then email your team a link to an anonymous survey. Or you can leave the group call for 30-minutes, and have them type their ideas into a shared document. They will come up with better feedback when working together so this second option will give better results.

Get a Gift, Give a Gift

If feedback is a gift, we shouldn't keep it to ourselves. Our employees want feedback, and we're in a position to gift it to them. I've never met an employee who didn't want to know if they were doing a good job. In fact, I've heard horror stories of employees who never got a review.

"Would you prefer to get feedback?" I ask them. They always say yes.

"I want to know what I'm doing well and how I can improve," they say.

Despite this, many leaders are convinced their staff doesn't want to hear from them. They think employees dread performance reviews, and they're doing their team a favor by skipping them. It's actually quite the opposite.

Telling the truth is the kindest thing you can do for someone. This is especially true when providing feedback. Almost everyone has a shortage of truth tellers in their life who are willing to say what no one else will.

I'm not talking about friends who tell you your tie doesn't match your shirt. I know you don't want to be a fashion disaster, but I'm thinking about more heartfelt things. I'm remembering Jim from the last chapter—the employee whose drinking got him passed over for promotions—aside from a quiet chat. I told him his habit of having "too much fun" was affecting his career. That was an ugly sweater feedback gift. It hurt him to hear it, and it wasn't fun to say. But it was a gift, and he could choose how to use it—or not.

The Personal Review Report Card

When I started giving structured feedback to my employees, I felt lost. I wasn't sure what to say. Now, I frame the meetings around a one-page Personal Review Report Card. Leaders love this report card. I introduce the idea of giving frequent feedback to their team, and they roll their eyes, thinking, Great. Another thing I have to do. But then the report card comes to the rescue.

Here's how it works: Every six months you schedule a one-on-one meeting with each of your direct reports. Sixty minutes is plenty of time. Before you meet, send each employee a Personal Review Report Card. This is a one-page document with six questions for the employee to answer. To be clear, you do not complete this. The prep work is all on the employee. That's why leaders love it.

Below are the six questions, and you can download a free copy of the report card at BalancedIQ.com.

1. List the top three goals in your previous review and describe your progress towards them.

2. What accomplishment are you most proud of since your last review? Consider the early part of this period as well as more recent events.

3. List any difficulties you have in carrying out your work. Are there any obstacles outside your control that prevent you from performing effectively?

4. What parts of your job do you feel you:
   - Do best?
   - Have difficulty with?

5. As your leader, what can I...
   - Do more of?
   - Do less of?

6. List two work-related goals and one personal goal you want to achieve. You must be able to measure them.

Top Tips for Your Meeting

Going through the report card together is an easy way to structure your meeting. As a guide, you should spend 10 percent of your time reviewing the employee's performance since the last review. The next 20 percent should go to reviewing the employee's previous top three goals and providing feedback. In the remaining 70 percent of your time, you should focus on developing a plan to make their future goals successful.

You'll notice this doesn't give you much time to talk about all the things the employee did wrong since their last review. This is intentional. You'll quickly discover employees are usually too hard on themselves. They don't need you to go on about all they've done wrong.

You may also have noticed the last item on the report card is a personal goal for your employee. What's with that? Aren't we talking about work? Yes, but we know when we achieve one goal, we become more motivated to accomplish another. We also know people who are happier in life, perform better at work. I see this happen time and time again. If my employee achieves their personal goal, they will also meet their work goal.

That's why I make my employees' personal goals as important as their work ones. They might want to buy a house by September, or lose 10 pounds, for example. We break the goal down. How much will you save from each paycheck for your down payment? What kind of salad will you have for lunch?

At the end of your report card meeting, schedule a 15-minute check-in every month. Yes, every month. You won't need any paperwork for these quick sessions. They're just an opportunity for one-on-one time with your employee. In those conversations, you'll ask how things are going, and your interest will earn their loyalty.

In a Harvard Business School MBA study on goal setting, they found that eighty-four percent of students that had written goals were making twice as much as the ones that had no written goals. Repeat the Personal Review Report Card meeting every six months, and schedule it in so doesn't get forgotten. You'll quickly find your team is committed to exceeding the goals that they created for themselves.

One quick note

This Personal Review Report Card will help you give the gift of feedback to your team, but if you need to have a serious conversation about, say, a code of ethics violation, use the guidance in chapter 16 instead. Code of ethics violations include things like harassment, repeated safety violations, inappropriate use of the internet, criminal activities, insubordination, and use of alcohol or illegal substances at work. There's a bigger list in chapter sixteen, along with step-by-step instructions to manage these situations.

♥ Take Action

1. What's your natural reaction to feedback, both positive and negative?

2. How will you conduct your personal engagement survey? Schedule it and invite your team.

3. Schedule Personal Review Report Card meetings with each of your direct reports, and download the report card from BalancedIQ.com.

P2: Positive Accountability

Where the Magic Happens!

[9]

THE POSITIVITY EFFECT

"There is no elevator to success, you have to take the stairs."

—Zig Ziglar, salesman, author, and motivational speaker.

There's an episode of the classic TV show Friends in which the gang throws a New Year's Eve party. Monica and Rachel's apartment is packed with holiday decorations, party music is blaring, and everyone's having a blast. There's drinking, dancing, and good times.

Then, we hear a knock on the door. The friends jump up, ecstatic. "Fun Bobby's here!" Monica opens the door and finds her boyfriend, Fun Bobby, standing there, shoulders slumped, looking desperately sad. His grandfather just died.

Soon, the music is silenced, and all the guests are gathered around Fun Bobby, as he describes the funeral arrangements.

"It's going to be an open casket," he says. "So at least I'll see him again." Someone passes a box of tissues around the crying crowd.

We've all seen it happen. When one person in the room feels down, they bring everyone else down with them. Negativity kills the party. It's contagious. It spreads from one person to the next and, while it might be appropriate at the news of a beloved grandfather's death, it can be very detrimental in the workplace.

Positivity Wins

We don't just know this from TV sitcoms and our own experiences; there's plenty of research proving negativity affects everything we do in a... wait for it... negative way. Harvard Business Review summed up the boat-load of research nicely when it said,

"A large and growing body of research on positive organizational psychology demonstrates that... a positive environment will lead to dramatic benefits for employers, employees, and the bottom line."

It detailed all the dots that are proven by studies to connect to positive workplaces to positive emotions, improved relationships, amplified creativity, better health, and increased loyalty to the leader and the organization. It went on to say,

"When organizations develop positive, virtuous cultures they achieve significantly higher levels of organizational effectiveness—including financial performance, customer satisfaction, productivity, and employee engagement."

The gains from creating a positive workplace aren't small beans, either. If you ask your company's human resources manager about healthcare benefits, they'll probably treat you to an extended rant on how expensive the program is. Well, high-stress companies spend nearly 50 percent more on health care than their chilled-out cohorts.

Can you imagine the effect on a country if all its businesses reduced employee stress and spent 50 percent less on health care? I'm not just talking about the premiums savings, either. The American Psychological Association estimates that stress costs the US economy more than $500 billion every year. Their statistics show stress is to blame for 80 percent of workplace accidents, more than 80% of doctors visits, and 550 million workdays lost each year.

Negative work environments also cause disengagement over the long term. This isn't necessarily true with smaller time frames. We can imagine—or have maybe experienced ourselves—a scenario where the manager puts the pressure on with crazy targets and tight deadlines, and we respond by knuckling down and hustling hard. We might even feel driven and excited by an overly-ambitious goal placed upon us.

This response doesn't last, though. Research suggests cut-throat environments cause inevitable stress, which will lead to disengagement over the long term. It is simply not a sustainable way of persuading employees to perform their best.

The *Harvard Business Review* identified a third cost of negative work environments which I know will interest you. It said,

"Workplace stress leads to an increase of almost fifty percent in voluntary turnover."

Turnover is a Problem

Turnover is a problem for so many leaders. If you're experiencing high turnover in your team, you're not alone, and it's no surprise you're frustrated with it. In the next part of this book, P3: Performance Accountability, we'll talk about reducing turnover in more detail, but it's important to recognize you can significantly influence this by creating a more positive environment.

Many workplace studies, including those assessed by Harvard Business Review, focus on stress, but research draws a pretty straight line from an increase in positivity to a decrease in stress. We don't need doctors and labs filled with mice to tell us this. Think back to the last time you felt stressed to the core. Were you positive and upbeat about it, humming a happy melody as anxiety crippled you from within? Of course not.

This line between positivity and reduced stress goes both ways, though. If you minimize stress in your life and work, you will feel more positive. But you don't need to rely on that. You can use positivity to decrease stress for yourself and your employees. In turn, you'll improve your team's performance, have a healthier and happier workforce, and boost your bottom line.

My dad didn't know how to use positivity. He taught me lots of great things in life—including accountability—but he did it in a negative way. That's why it took me more than three decades to appreciate him. He taught me well but, without positivity, it took me a long time to recognize those lessons.

We don't have three decades to learn the lessons research is teaching us today. As leaders, we want to create better-performing workplaces, so we must be held accountable for creating positive environments. That's why the second P in the 3Ps program is Positive Accountability, and that's what we're delving into now.

Over the next few chapters, we'll review three powerful ways to foster a positive work environment. The remainder of this chapter focuses on positive language. In the next, we'll discuss creating positive experiences for employees. Then, we'll dive into positively magnifying small wins at work.

Let's get into it with the number one way you can foster a positive work environment: your language.

Positive language

Using positive language uplifts your mood and the mood of whoever you're talking to. It makes you appear more confident, likable, and trustworthy. You also get better and faster results because you're less likely to offend people. When you choose your words with care, you avoid unnecessary confrontations and time taken away from your primary goals.

We can see this with a short comparison exercise. Read the following statements and note how each makes you feel. See if any of them triggers a change in your mood.

- I have to go for a run.
- I want to go for a run.

- I can't do this.
- I won't do this.

- I should watch my kids play soccer.
- I'd like to watch my kids play soccer.

- I understand your point, but we need to make it this way.
- I understand your point, and we need to make it this way.

I don't know about you, but in each pairing, the second statement makes me feel more in control, empowered, and excited. It makes me less likely to be stubborn and rebellious. In each example, just a small change in word choice triggered an improved reaction in me.

Replaced:
- I have with I *want*;
- I can't with I *won't*;
- I should with *I'd like to*;
- but with *and.*

You can use small tweaks like these to improve how others respond to you. There are a few more business-specific examples of negative language which can be switched out for positive, that I'd like to share with you.

Acquired

I've dealt with a lot of change, mergers, and acquisitions in my time. When I'd go into a new company we'd just acquired, I'd discover the employees weren't feeling great about it. Not only were they afraid of the changes to come, but they felt disempowered. I could see it on their faces. Knowing they'd been "acquired" made them feel like property, subject to the whims of whoever now owns them.

I learned to say merged instead of acquired. Merged suggests a partnership. Whatever the finer details of the new corporate structure, ensuring your employees feel like people in a partnership, not property, is essential.

Change

When you hear your pay is being changed, you freak out. When the head office announces changes to your operating procedures, you instantly think you'll have to put in overtime. Change = bad.

Logically, we know this isn't always true. Pay raises happen. Switching your vehicle from an old, beat-up toaster on wheels to a new, fun sports car is a great change. Occasionally, new operating procedures actually make life easier. But as human beings, our instinct is to fear change.

My colleagues and I found that promising to change things always caused friction, but when we said we'd improve things, people jumped on board. It almost didn't matter what we were suggesting if it was an improvement, not a change. As we almost always make changes to improve, we can usually use these words interchangeably. Steer clear of changes, though, as improvements always get a better response. Remember: Change = Improvements.

If you're having a hard time seeing changes as improvements, remember the caterpillar. These little bugs travel less than a mile in their caterpillar form. Then, they undergo a massive change. They become a butterfly, and with their big, beautiful wings, they can migrate over three thousand miles. Big changes—or improvements, rather— can take you far.

Problems

When people hear about problems, human nature makes them focus on protecting themselves. So how do you discuss problems at work without your employees sinking into self-preservation mode? You call them challenges.

"We have a challenge we need to make improvements on," you say.

Negative language, like talking about problems, will make them stop listening so they can focus on saving their skins. On the other hand, challenges are engaging. They don't carry the same negative connotations. They encourage employees to jump in and overcome the challenge at hand.

Why

Why is an attacking word. Why did you do that? Why did you think that was a good idea? It makes a person feel under fire, which makes them defensive. When your employee is busy defending their actions, they have less time and energy to create solutions.

This might be tricky because there will inevitably be times when you do want to know why your employee did something. Instead of asking the direct question, you'll get a better response by saying, "Tell me more about that." We used this technique in the Personal Engagement Survey from the last chapter because it encourages employees to speak openly.

Replace the question, "Why didn't you think about..." with, "Did you consider...?" These rephrased questions will prompt your employees to brainstorm. The conversations will be less direct and may take longer, but you'll get the result you need. Your employee will engage in the challenge being discussed and perform better moving forward.

Let's Not Sugarcoat

I want to clarify something before we move on. Being positive does not mean sugarcoating negative situations. There are going to be challenges you'll need to communicate with your team. Sometimes, you'll have to talk about difficult things. That's because you're the leader.

You owe it to your employees to tell them what they need to know, which might not be what they want to hear.

It is possible to do this and be positive at the same time, even when the message itself isn't great. You just need to be conscious of the language you use and speak with well-considered honesty.

Well-considered honesty means you tell the truth while carefully considering what you say. You might not need to share the high-level details of the company decision, just as parents don't share every household problem with their kids.

Whatever is appropriate to share, you should share honestly. You don't need to embellish a disastrous situation to scare your team into performing better. You also shouldn't exaggerate, making things appear better or worse. Your employees might discover the truth from another source, and learn to distrust you.

Consider what you share with your team. Retain trust by remaining honest. Drop unnecessary use of negative words. Then, you'll create a high-performing workplace through positive language. It's not a fast-track to success; it takes effort to train yourself to use more positive language. But as Zig Ziglar says, "There's no elevator to success, you have to take the stairs." You can take the stairs one word at a time. Before you know it, you'll be miles higher than ever before.

♥ Take Action

1. Do you think your coworkers see you as a positive or negative person?

2. Starting using positive words with others. What is the response and how does it make you feel?

3. Write down the negative words you frequently use, and the positive words you'll use instead.

[10]

POSITIVE EXPERIENCES

"People may hear your words, but they feel your attitude."

—John C. Maxwell, leadership expert, author, and speaker.

I love playing golf. It's a challenging sport, and it's taught me a lot of lessons about life. The hardest shots on a golf course are those with a big obstacle, like a tree, sand trap, ravine, or the dreaded water. For some reason, my balls used to love diving into water. It was like they were magnetically attracted there, no matter how I hit the ball.

One day, I read some simple advice on a golf blog. It said, "Think about the outcome you want, not what you don't want." I realized I'd always played water hazards in the same way. I mean, I was constantly adjusting my angles and my swing, but every shot began with the same process... I'd line myself up at the tee, see the pond blocking my path to the hole, look down at my ball, back to the pond, and think, I hate water hazards. I fixated on the obstacle, not the path past it.

I learned the best way to keep a ball from drowning was to imagine the outcome I wanted for it. I had to visualize hitting the ball, and, in my mind's eye, see it soaring over the water, landing cleanly on the green. This simple mental trick worked wonders. The more I practiced visualizing my shots, the more my balls found their way past water hazards.

Of course, it's not enough just to visualize your game and expect to win without any other action. I still had to pick up the club, be conscious of my stance, and remember the movements that make for proper form. But when all that wasn't enough, visualizing a positive experience on that hole helped me create a good experience.

Visualizing the outcome you want, and focusing on the potential positive experience, not the negative, is a concrete step towards achieving that positive outcome. It's a time-tested technique used by top sporting pros, as well as weekend golf hacks like me.

Back in the 1960s, tennis legend Billie Jean King used visualization to prepare for the many, many matches she won. Decades later, Olympic teams across the world have sports psychologists on board to help athletes imagine success in their events. During the 2014 Winter Games, *The New York Times* reported a whole gaggle of sports psychologists showed in Sochi. Team USA had nine;

Canada, eight; Norway, three. By the time the flame was passed on in the closing ceremonies, those nations all ranked in the top four medal-winners.

Visualizing Positive Work Experiences

Business leaders may not be pushing their bodies to the extremes reached by Olympians, and my golf swing isn't quite Championship-worthy yet, but we can all use visualization to step-up our game. Picturing a positive work environment will help you create it. Likewise, focusing on how lousy your team is or how poorly they're performing will reinforce that negativity.

Fixating on the negative stuff is easy. When you collapse on the sofa after dinner, those issues that riled you up during the day can come back to the forefront. You find yourself going around in circles about that thing so-and-so said, or how your team will never be able to meet those targets.

But you must visualize the outcome you want—a positive work environment that leads to improved performance. Take time to picture what that looks like. Imagine your team members' enthusiastic attitudes as you talk to them. In your mind's eye, see the improved sales numbers on your computer screen. Read the email from your leader congratulating your department's stellar efforts. Sink into the feeling that comes when you know you're doing a great job.

Then, go into work the next day ready to make that imagery scenario a reality. Keep the picture in mind, so you know what you're aiming for, and come back to it often.

This small mindset trick will help you focus on creating a positive work environment.

In the last chapter, we discussed the benefits of positive work environments and the power that positive language has to create them. Being conscientious of our words is the easiest way to create positivity, but the old saying remains true: Actions speak louder than words. We need to support our upbeat language with real action.

When you sharpen your focus by picturing your success, and take action to enact those visualizations, you can create a work environment that your employees treasure. Turnover rates will plummet because your team will want to be at work. At the same time, performance will skyrocket as employees become motivated to give their all.

So... How Does This Work, Exactly?

The real question is this: How do you get from where you are, where nothing is jiving and everything's an uphill battle, to that imagined successful environment where everyone loves their job, their exceeding their professional goals, birds sing merrily, the sun always shines, and rainbows and unicorns dance on your desk?

Well first, "success" doesn't have to involve rainbows and unicorns. You're the leader. You're the one visualizing the future. You get to choose what it looks like. It may feel like your work environment revolves around luck—or a lack of it. In fact, you have the power to determine what a successful workplace looks like for you and your team. Play with this when you visualize your success, and know you can control the outcome.

Second, there are many different actions you can take to create positivity at work. Below are some examples I've used which I encourage you to replicate. Or, take inspiration from them to come up with your own ideas. The best options are those that naturally appeal to you (as that's a sign they fit well with your personality), and those that match up with your employees' interests and inclinations.

It may feel, at first, like none of these options are natural to you. If you read through the suggestions below and aren't drawn to any, ask yourself why. It may just be because this is new, and it takes time to get comfortable with new behaviors.

When, in my mid-30s, I decided to start telling my parents I love them, it didn't come naturally. It was awkward and felt forced. But I persevered, and now I say, "I love you" at the end of every call with my mom as if I'd been saying it all my life. It's no longer weird; it makes me feel good. Pick the least awful ideas below, put them into action, and persevere.

Actions to Create Positive Experiences

Praising employees in front of others

It's good for your ego when your leader praises you. It's an even bigger boost when they do it in front of an audience. I noticed if I grabbed my leader in the break room and told him about Helen's success, while Helen sat there listening, it was a big deal to her. She'd be proud of that moment. When I announced that James had done a great job that week so he would be choosing where the team went for lunch, James glowed.

Praising employees in front of others, especially to those more senior, is a really effective tactic that costs nothing but a few minutes of your time. You can do it off the cuff, when you and your employee pass the CEO in the corridor, or more formally, for example, taking the first two minutes of your team's big presentation to praise their efforts in putting it together. Even better, you'll find both informal and formal opportunities to make a big deal out of your employees' successes.

Giving out thank you notes

When my team was putting in overtime, I'd write a thank you note to the spouse and mail it to their home. It'd just have a few lines saying something like, Many thanks for letting your husband be here. He's very important to our team and we'll make it up to you both soon. I knew the employee would read the note as well. The words weren't particularly profound, but they always went over well.

Thank you notes can be delivered in other ways, too. It can be a simple text message. This new era of employees love that. I don't recommend texting for most communication; it's hard to goal set, give action items, or have disciplinary discussions that way. But praise is easier to communicate. Just say you're checking in, are wondering how they're doing, and want to say thank you for [whatever you're specifically thanking them for].

Personal, company- and department-wide emails, physical notes left on someone's desk, mentions in meetings, and tags accompanying gifts are other great ways of giving out thank you's.

Sending personalized gifts

When we started getting aggressive with our sales targets at Sleep Train, people thought we were crazy. To meet these stretched goals, we did an intensive year selling the Fab Five: mattresses, foundations, pillows, protectors, and sheets on each customer order. My team put in a lot of hours to hit the mark. I sent chocolate-covered strawberries to each of their homes so, when they exceeded the monthly target in each of the Fab Five, they could share a treat with their families. The card that came with the strawberries was perfect for a short thank you note for their sweet success. Their families motivated the employee to repeat the performance again, which caused our sales to go viral (in a great way).

Any kind of personalized gift is effective because it shows you appreciate the employee both for their work and for who they are as an individual. It demonstrates you've noticed their efforts, and seen who they are as a person.

In contrast, a generic gift card is the worst thing you can give. One of those reloadable credit card vouchers you can get from any gas station doesn't exactly scream, Saw this and thought of you! It says, I couldn't be bothered to think of something personal, and this was quick to grab. Your employee might like the credit, but it won't create the kind of impactful, positive experience that will improve the atmosphere at work.

For inspired personalized gift ideas, get to know your employees' hobbies. If you have a team member with a green thumb, you could get them a decent set of hedge clippers for a hundred bucks. A friend of mine had a whiskey-drinking ceremony incorporated into her wedding service, so her leader sent the newlyweds a bottle of Scotch. Speaking on behalf of all golfers, we love a round at the local course.

For many people, their "hobby" is family. That's their focus in their precious time outside of work. Giving something to an employee's child is a fun twist on the hobby-based idea. You could send a gift card for a movie theater, addressed to little Jonnie, with a note asking him to take mom and dad out. Parents, myself included, love that stuff.

More practical gifts go down well, too. A single mom might love a voucher for a few hours from a house cleaner. A sports massage for your team member with a strained calf muscle could be perfect.

Gifts don't have to be extra-curricular. Turning off an employee's email while they're on vacation is a practical, work-related, and completely free gift that is always appreciated. Just be sure to let the employee know what you've done, so they don't worry there's a technical glitch.

Spending time together

Spending relaxed time with your team is a wonderfully positive experience for both leaders and employees. We're not talking about complicated or overly time-consuming events, here. Bringing staff into your home for few drinks, a barbeque, and a round of Charades, if that's your thing, is one evening of effort that gives a huge return.

Keep it simple, invite your employees' partners, and have a theme. Themes like "ugly sweater party" or "super heroes" provide easy talking points and help everyone know what to expect. Make it something you're interested in, and don't overthink it. A good rule is to treat your employees like a S.T.A.R.: Something They Always Remember.

It's Worth The Investment

Visualizing and taking action to create positive experiences at work will improve the atmosphere more than you think possible. The positive words we focused on in the last chapter are essential but, as leadership expert John C. Maxwell said, "People will hear your words, but they'll feel your attitude." The visualization and actions we just went through will create a positive attitude your employees will feel.

Yes, it takes some cash to give gifts, host drinks, and make people feel appreciated. However, it's an investment in your team, and it will be significantly lower than the cost of high turnover. Once you get into it, you'll also find this is a fun tactic that will leave you feeling inspired. It's not just a positive experience for the employee, but for you, too.

You can, and should, expand this concept into your business activities. Day-to-day tasks like setting sales targets can be positive and fun experiences, too. That's what we'll explore in the next chapter.

♥ Take Action

1. Which positive experiences already exist in your workplace?

2. Are there positive experiences that can be better personalized, if so, how?

3. Visualize a more positive work environment. Imagine it in detail, using all your senses. What do you see as you look around? What does the atmosphere feel like? What do you hear people saying? Repeat this exercise for a few minutes every day.

Tip: Go to BalancedIQ.com and download the extended list of positive experience ideas. Highlight the best ones for your workplace, and make a plan to take action on them.

CELEBRATE SMALL WINS

"Track your small wins to motivate big accomplishments."

—Dr Teresa Amabile, professor of Business Administration in the Entrepreneurial Management Unit, Harvard Business School.

I took my daughter, Carmina, to the golf range for the first time when she was eight years old. I was excited to share my favorite hobby with her and wanted her to do well. In my eagerness to create the golf prodigy I never was, I coached her hard. I thought, If I stay on her and ensure she learns right from the start, she'll be in good shape. She won't have to unlearn bad habits as I did, losing many balls from my ugly slice. So that afternoon, I corrected every swing and told her how to adjust each angle. She hated it. On the way home, she said she'd never go back. She didn't want to hit balls ever again. I was devastated, as I'd so wanted to play golf with my daughter.

Fast forward three years. My son, Riley, was seven, and he asked to go to the driving range with me. I was determined to learn from my mistakes with Carmina, so I handed Riley the club, gave him the basics on how to swing, and let him go at it. Every time he made contact with the ball, we celebrated. I didn't coach him at all. We just whooped and high-fived any time he hit the ball. It was fun for both of us, and the drive home was a lot happier than the one with Carmina three years prior.

That evening, as always, we did our Family Dinner Favorites. We go around the table, and each raise a toast to our favorite part of the day. Riley raised his glass of milk and said, "Cheers to hitting golf balls... my favorite part of the day!" Carmina, now 11-years-old, heard this and asked if I'd take her next time. I jumped on this second chance with my daughter and took both the kids to the driving range the very next day.

This time, I did the same as I'd done with Riley. We celebrated all the small wins, every time Carmina made contact with the ball. I was pleasantly surprised by how well she did. We had a great day together, and Carmina stuck with it. She made the varsity golf team as a freshman and played in a variety of junior golf tournaments. We still play together, too. Some of the most special moments in my free time are while playing golf with my kids, and it's what I always ask for on Father's Day. It's amazing how encouraging Carmina's small wins ended with such big, meaningful results for both of us.

Celebrating Small Wins at Work

I experienced something similar in the work world, particularly when I was at Sleep Train. For years, we didn't have a director of human resources (HR). The various department leaders just shot from the hip on how to manage HR. We did the best we could with what we knew—or thought we knew—about recruiting, managing, and sometimes firing people. But as the company grew, our founder, Dale, in his wisdom, saw we needed help. He went out and hired Tracy Jackson, an HR professional with more than a decade of experience.

Now, at that time, we were primarily a "guys" company. In our ignorance, we hadn't given any attention to diversity. We didn't know, back then, all the benefits that come from a more balanced workforce. So when Dale announced we'd have to answer to an HR manager, I'm ashamed to say our collective thought was, Uh oh. There was a lot of talk around the water cooler. We bemoaned the extra hoops she'd no doubt force us to jump through. We complained about all the red tape she'd surely strangle us with.

In our first executive team meeting, Tracy and I sat across from each other in the board room. I leaned back in my chair, arms crossed, surveying her as she gestured enthusiastically and spoke with real passion. She said there is no template. Human resources is about humans, and we have to stay consistent while realizing no two employees are the same. It's about people, first and foremost. In minutes, I found myself leaning forward, listening intently, my hesitation flying out the window. I was impressed. Tracy quickly proved herself to be unbelievably good at the job. She won over everyone, and taught us what we should've already realized: Having a woman in the room only improves things, and giving proper attention to HR issues creates more engaged employees.

We developed a great relationship. Tracy expertly guided me through many sticky moments and helped me become a better leader. So, 11 years later, when Tracy said she couldn't relocate her family to move to the company's new headquarters in Texas, I was gutted. The team understood, of course, but we were all sad. Tracy got a new job which would allow her to stay in the area, but before she left, she undertook a small, personal challenge she called Losing My Marbles.

She bought a bag of marbles and set a goal to give each marble to a colleague who'd made a difference in her career. She put them all in a bowl on her desk and said seeing them there held her personally accountable to fulfilling her goal. Only when the bowl was empty would she know she'd accomplished what she'd wanted, and thanked the people who'd meant something to her. A couple of times a day, she took a marble from the bowl, handed it to someone in the office, and spent two or three minutes thanking them for their help. It became very symbolic.

When she brought a marble into my office, she sat down across the desk from me, just as she'd done in that first meeting. She talked about how I'd leaned on her in my career—which was very true, and how that had helped her see the meaning in her work. She said my trust had helped her develop. I'd had no idea! She had done more for me than I'd ever done for anyone else, and it was so encouraging to hear our relationship had benefited her. It was a small gesture that celebrated a mutual win, and it encouraged me beyond measure. That moment stayed with me. And I never lost my marble; it stayed with me, too.

Small Wins Demolish Walls

Tracy's example reminded me of something I did a few years prior. I'd realized every time I showed up in a colleague's cubicle, I was asking them for something. I wondered if I could build better relationships by showing up to give. But what would I give? Office supplies? Extra staples? No one wanted those. But there is something that's almost universally appreciated: candy.

I bought a case of 100 Grand candy bars and started handing them out. I didn't just dump them in a bowl in the office kitchen, though. I gave them out one by one, with a thank you for a specific achievement. Sometimes, I said something meaningful. Other times, I kept it simple and light, and just said, "You've worked so hard. Here's your payday... one hundred grand!" It went down well. It's amazing how much people will help you when you've shown up to give. I expanded my efforts and bought a bunch of Take 5 candy bars. In the morning, I'd put six on my desk and challenge myself to give them all out before I could take a break. I continued the cheesy wordplay, and told team members, "Take five! You've done a great job. You deserve a break."

My relationships improved, people were more willing to help me, and I felt good for it. Finding excuses to give out the candy bars made me notice all the small wins my team scored. It was encouraging to see. When I shared the moment with a team member, and we celebrated a small win together, they were encouraged, too. The positive experience was contagious.

I took my efforts on the road when I visited stores in my region. I'd always felt store staff were intimidated when head office leaders came in. It was like they put up a wall to protect themselves because they were sure you were there to tell them they'd done wrong. But when I went in and found small wins to celebrate, right off the bat, that wall disappeared. I handed out candy bars, chocolates, and snacks. I'd say, "These are your sales vitamins. When you're having a bad day, eat them!" Then, they opened up. We had real, productive conversations.

It was such a change from the audit programs I used to do. When I started visiting mattress stores, I wanted to catch the staff off guard. I'd turn up without much notice, put on a white glove, and run my finger over the headboards, looking for dust. I'd review every aspect and, many times, found stores weren't up to par. They weren't organized enough, clean enough, welcoming enough, whatever. I'd only get through two or three stores in one trip because it took so much time to audit them fully.

When I shifted my mentality, I decided to give the district leader two week's notice before showing up. The leader would use the visit to motivate the staff to get the store spotless. Instead of donning my white glove as soon as I arrived, I asked the team to show me the store. They started talking to me, telling me their wins and what they wished they could do better. I got some resistance from higher leaders who thought we should catch what they do when we're not there. But the results spoke for themselves. In follow-ups, I found they maintained a clean, welcoming store throughout the summer—our busiest months.

I also went home happier. My days were more enjoyable when I wasn't being a Hernazi. I knew I'd helped improve our service standards, I'd enveloped so many more leaders into taking ownership of and pride in the state of our stores, and I was able to see more stores in one trip. My top goal was to motivate the staff and get them more excited about our company. Win, win, win.

Small Wins in the Big Picture

Celebrating small wins, like hitting a ball or meeting all your store's cleanliness criteria, is one thing. Bigger wins, such as exceeding sales targets, are more difficult to reward. Offering a chocolate bar to celebrate six months of long hours slaving over sales numbers just won't cut it. But the same principle applies: You need to track small wins as you work towards bigger goals.

Breaking big tasks into a series of small ones isn't a new idea, of course. How do you eat an elephant? One bite at a time. It's common for annual sales targets to be broken down into quarterly, monthly, and weekly goals per district, and individual branch. The point is that it's not enough to set these smaller, milestone goals. You must celebrate them, too. You need to use those smaller targets as opportunities to magnify the wins along the way, so your team has enough motivation to make it to the finish line. Without celebration, it just feels like one target comes after another, after another, and no success is ever enough. That's miserable and demoralizing, and that feeling slows everyone down.

Magnifying small wins with micro-celebrations creates momentum. It boosts morale and motivation, and speeds everything up. It's a classic tortoise and hare situation. By taking time out to celebrate a small win, you get to your final destination faster. And remember, that time out doesn't have to last long. Tracy took two or three minutes to thank her colleagues. It took me no more than that to pass out candy bars. High-fiving Carmina took her away from the tee for five seconds.

At Sleep Train, we used weekly sales targets, as your company might. Week in, week out, these numbers helped us monitor our progress towards the larger, annual goals. We also used them, every single week, to magnify our top salespeople. We praised those who hit the weekly targets. We didn't shame those who didn't, but we let them see those goals were possible because their teammate was doing it. It helped them understand that hitting those numbers was an attainable goal, and it was the kind of thing that was regularly praised around here.

Using Self-Imposed Checkpoints

When our executive leadership team created ambitious targets for us to exceed, we created checkpoints as opportunities to magnify our salespeople and their wins. You can create these for any goal you want your team to achieve, whatever the measurement looks like. Here's an example of how we did it when we wanted to lower our exchange rate.

As most retail stores do, we offered an exchange option. Customers could take a mattress home, try it for one hundred days, and exchange it if they didn't love it. Allowing exchanges is vital to gain customer trust and loyalty, but exchanges cost the company money. We set a company-wide goal of lowering our exchange rate from 18 percent to 10 percent. We didn't have a fixed time frame, but even without that pressure, it was a big goal.

We broke the target down into three checkpoints. The first was at 30 percent of the total goal. We were aiming for an overall reduction of 8 percentage points, and 30 percent of 8 is 2.4. We took our current rate of 18 percent, subtracted 2.4 percent, and got our first checkpoint target of a 15.6 percent exchange rate. This 30 percent goal should be a quick and easy win for the whole team, which creates momentum. From there, we magnified the early sprinters and encouraged the others.

The second checkpoint was at 70 percent of the end goal. The math was the same: 70 percent of 8 is 5.6 percent. From the original 18 percent, we subtracted 5.6 percent, to get a 70 percent goal of a 12.4 percent exchange rate. Our top performers hit the 70 percent goal fairly quickly. That created a positive atmosphere, with the rest of the team seeing those wins were possible. When we praised the top performers, the rest of the team were encouraged to follow along. Seeing their teammates accomplish a goal they had thought was unattainable gave them the confidence to get on board and get selling, so they wouldn't be left behind. It was powerful social proof, which is a type of conformity. When a person is unsure how to behave, for example, if they should pursue a goal that seems out of reach, they often look to others for clues concerning the correct behavior. Is it right to slack off, since the goal is unrealistic anyway? Or is the correct behavior to go after the goal?

The final checkpoint was the original goal of a 10 percent exchange rate. With some training and detailed performance measurements, we achieved this final checkpoint of a 10 percent exchange rate fairly quickly. Those 8 percentage points saved the company about $8 million a year. Breaking such an audacious goal into smaller chunks made it seem more realistic. Eating one-third of an elephant is less intimidating than eating the whole thing. You go one bite at a time and celebrate at each checkpoint to keep your momentum. With the savings we made that year, we paid out some great staff bonuses. It was a lot of fun.

How to Celebrate Small Wins

For examples of easy, fun things I've done to celebrate team members' small wins, look back at the list of positive experiences in the last chapter. These same ideas you used to create general positive experiences can also magnify the small wins of specific employees. After all, celebrating small wins should, quite simply, be a positive experience! Steal those ideas, or use any others that honor your employees.

Whatever you choose to do to celebrate small wins, it's worth it. Rewards—verbal encouragement, symbolic marbles, candy, or anything else—motivate people to reach bigger goals. A high-five when your daughter hits a golf ball can encourage her to put in the effort required to become a varsity golfer. I'm not saying I'm responsible for Carmina's success—that's all on her. I just realized that, when I didn't celebrate her small wins, I created a barrier that prevented her from pushing on. I sucked all the joy from the driving range, and who wants to do something that's not enjoyable?

Recognizing small wins was a habit I had to cultivate, but it's a habit that snowballs. As soon as you start noticing the great things your team is doing, it becomes easier to see even more. It very quickly turns from a chore to improve your team's performance, to a fun exercise you enjoy doing, that also benefits your team. As Dr Teresa Amabile from Harvard Business School said, "Track your small wins to motivate big accomplishments." And the fun thing is, you never know how big those accomplishments will be!

♥ Take Action

1. Which small goals will you set, so your team can experience early wins?

2. How will you praise small wins and early top performers?

3. Communicate these goals at your next meeting and begin praising small wins. Keep it simple, and add a calendar reminder to do it weekly. You'll lose hearts if you don't follow up consistently.

P3: Performance Accountability

What You Permit, You Promote

[12]

SETTING EXPECTATIONS

"People can't live up to the expectations they don't know have been set for them."

—Rory Vaden, motivational speaker and New York Times best selling author.

Not long after Angie and I married, we bought our first home. I wanted a few plants for the backyard, so while we were at Home Depot buying curtain rods and tools, I headed over to the nursery section. I was bent over a display of purple-flowered Lily of the Niles, reading the labels, trying to figure out if they'd survive without full sun.

There was a sudden, sharp pain in the back of my leg. I wheeled around and saw a tiny kid—he couldn't have been more than three-years-old—looking up from the behind the shopping cart he'd just slammed into me. His dad came running over, saw the small, bloody gash on my calf, and apologized over and over.

I was annoyed. I mean, it hurt! But I told the man it was okay. I gave the kid a small smile and went back to picking out a plant. Later, I thought if it had been someone else pushing that cart, I would've reacted very differently. If it had been a teenager having a laugh and running around, or an adult who wasn't paying attention, I would've probably given them a few choice words about how to behave in public, or told him to watch where they're going.

But I hadn't said anything like that, because my assailant was a small child. I didn't have my own kids then, but I knew three-year-olds can't fully understand social expectations. That little boy had probably never been told it's not okay to slam shopping carts into stranger's legs, or that those wobbly wheels make it easy to lose control. He wasn't being willfully disobedient or disrespectful. He just didn't know the dangers of freewheeling around Home Depot.

Over the years, I've told that story to many leaders in many training programs. It's a reminder that before you react to a situation, you have to consider the expectations. Is the shopping cart-pusher the kind of person who should know better? Or is it someone who doesn't yet know what's expected of them in aisle ten of home furnishings?

The same is true for reacting to our employees. It's not fair to get mad at them for doing something they don't even know is wrong. Although expectations might seem obvious to you, you can't be surprised your staff doesn't meet them if you haven't taken the time to explicitly set them. You can't hold someone accountable when they haven't been properly trained.

Unconsciously Setting Expectations

When you don't openly and overtly communicate on this, it's easy to unintentionally set expectations. Telling a child that you expect them to go slow when pushing a shopping cart is pretty straightforward, but by the time we're adults in the workforce, communication is more complicated. Employees take their cues from general societal expectations, their new company's on-boarding brochures, the explicit instructions given to them, and, most notably, the examples set by their leaders and colleagues.

That's why we spent so much time talking about your personal accountability and leveling-up your own game before you look to your staff. If you're ten minutes late to work every morning, or if a team member is consistently late and you never hold them accountable for it, you set the expectation that tardiness is tolerated. If you permit poor punctuality, you promote it. You may never consciously say, "It's okay if you turn up late," but you say it through your behavior and your tolerance of other people's behavior.

It might be that you do set a good example of punctuality, and your team understands the unspoken, seemingly obvious rule that if your shift starts at 10am, you arrive ready to work at 10am. But when new employees come to us, they don't come from a vacuum. They've had previous experiences which all carried their own expectations.

They might have had a former leader who did permit them to roll up whenever they wanted. I've heard of people running late, calling their manager to let them know, and the manager using the employee's password (that they're not supposed to know) to clock the employee in. If your new team member comes from a leader who was complicit in getting away with being late, of course they won't expect you to be annoyed with their tardiness!

It does sound silly that you should have to tell adults to show up on time. If a previous leader, teacher, or parent ingrained certain behaviors in them, though, it's not their fault when they repeat them. At least, not if no one has taught them differently. Even adults who have been in the workforce for decades follow human nature and look around for non-verbal cues for how to behave in a new environment. The need to fit in comes from basic human survival instincts, and mimicking the behavior of others is how we fit in.

Obvious or Not-So-Obvious Expectations

After leading more than five thousand people, I've seen many seemingly obvious expectations become issues because they were not explicitly laid out. Below are some common employee behaviors I hear leaders complain about. They all stem from a lack of communication around what's expected.

- Poor timekeeping;
- Not meeting deadlines;

- Texting or emailing on a cell phone during meetings;
- Using work time for personal activities, like scrolling through social media, online shopping, or running personal errands;
- Failing to follow work delivery protocols;
- Looking "sloppy" or dressing too casually; or
- Using inappropriate language.

Of course, there are some things which we really do expect to be obvious, such as not engaging in illegal activities, or displaying violent, abusive, or disruptive behavior. In the coming chapters, we'll discuss how to handle these and other gross misconduct behaviors. It's worth noting, though, that you can't lose by communicating even the most basic expectations.

A friend of mine recently took the Canadian citizenship test. The immigration department provided a study guide to help her prepare. Within the first few pages of that guide, there was a warning for prospective new citizens: Spousal abuse, "honor" killings, and other gender-based violence will not be tolerated. Canada does not take it for granted that newcomers understand these expectations. Beneath that warning, the responsibilities of citizenship were listed. The first was that Canadians are required to obey the law. That should be obvious. But what does the country lose by explicitly stating that most basic requirement? It costs them half an inch of space in an online PDF.

Employees Love Expectations

Don't be afraid to communicate your expectations clearly. Employees love them! It clears any ambiguity or anxiety about how to fit in and how to succeed. Even when conversations around this are difficult, employees still appreciate them. I learned this from Scott Higgins, a Sleep Train team member with a lot of promise, whom I knew one day would lead a team of his own.

Scott was one of the "highly promising" team members I invited to attend our exclusive Management Training Program (MTP) one year. MTP was an intensive, classroom-based event that required pre-work. Well in advance, we sent all the attendees a workbook and instructed them to complete it before training started. We told them it was mandatory work.

Scott showed up for day one with his workbook only partially filled in. In the first break of the morning, I took Scott aside, heard all his excuses, and sent him home. He asked if he could complete the pre-work that night and come back the next day. I said no. We expected him to meet the original deadlines. He hadn't done that so he could not participate in this round of MTP. He'd have to wait for another invitation.

Fifteen years later, Scott admitted he'd been furious with me that morning. But he also said later that same day, he'd cooled off and realized it was his own fault his workbook wasn't done. After being booted out of a sure shot to management, it only took a few hours for him to appreciate that we set an expectation, and he didn't meet it. I invited Scott to the next round of MTP. He arrived with his pre-work complete, and went on to become an excellent leader. I was very fortunate to have him report directly to me for more than fifteen years.

Recently, Scott said, "When you have to hold someone accountable for their performance, the conversation should be very straightforward. They shouldn't be caught off guard. They should know they did something wrong before you even meet with them." To this day, Scott clearly sets expectations with anyone he works with. He follows up and does what he promises. As an employee, he appreciated clear and fulfilled expectations—even when they didn't work in his favor. As a leader, he makes it a priority to set and follow through on expectations for those around him. Scott has become a mentor and an expert in knowing how to create a high performing team.

Doing the Work in Order

Throughout this book, you've spent a lot of time thinking about your own behavior, and learning about P1: Personal Accountability. You explored what it means to have a hero mentality, like five-year-old Garrett who, after his terminal cancer diagnosis, took control of how he'd be remembered by planning the most fun superhero funeral ever. You considered how, as a leader, you are constantly being watched by your employees. You stepped up and gave yourself the gift of feedback through a personal engagement survey.

Then you took responsibility for P2: Positive Accountability. You learned the importance of using positive language at work and got ideas on how to create positive experiences for your team. I hope, by now, you've done at least one of those positive experiences, and felt the exponential benefit of them. You thought about how to magnify and celebrate small wins in your team, so they motivate employees to reach bigger goals. You've done a lot of work.

If you haven't done the work... if you skipped ahead to this section because it sounded best, if you lost your nerve and couldn't bring yourself to do the action items, or if you figured they weren't that important anyway, so you'd just read ahead, I want you to stop.

Stop right here.

Do you remember that commitment you made to yourself back in chapter one? You committed to using this process to turn things around at work. You acknowledged things weren't as good as you wanted them to be, but if you read this book and acted on its advice, you could see real changes in your organization. Just picking up this book was an act of engagement to create something better than before. You owe it to yourself to try, right?

If you're tempted to try the action items in this section, P3: Performance Accountability, before the earlier ones, you should know you're setting yourself up to fail. It won't work. It will be a waste of your time and effort, and might make you look foolish in the process. Performance Accountability is closer to traditional ideas about holding others accountable. Many people want to gloss over the earlier, seemingly harder stuff and jump straight into the more familiar concepts. But if you haven't set the right expectations through Personal and Positive Accountability, you'll have no authority when you try to implement Performance Accountability. Your staff won't care.

Raising the Bar

If you do step up to the challenge and lay the groundwork, P3: Performance Accountability will be the easiest step. I promise! You will have created such a positive and accountable environment that you won't have to discipline staff so often. You'll be able to move away from being a "gotcha" manager—catching them when they're doing wrong, and move into being a coach for top performers. You'll be able to set expectations from a new recruit's first moments, and turn your existing employees from lackluster to the dream team. You'll be confident in dealing with unexpected and unforgivable behavior, and you'll be a driving force to help people become greater than themselves. We'll explore all this in the upcoming chapters.

When you set expectations, you're not just providing backup for any disciplinary actions further down the line. It's not just about covering your butt. We're talking about engaging your employees' hearts and minds and proactively raising the standard of their work. As Rory Vaden, the motivational speaker and *The New York Times* bestselling author, says, "People can't live up to the expectations they don't know have been set for them." If you want your team to meet—or exceed—your expectations, they must first know what they are. It's your responsibility to communicate them, and ensure everyone is professionally accountable.

♥ Take Action

1. What expectations have you openly already set for your team?

2. What unconscious expectations have you set for them, through your own behavior or through permitting other people's behavior?

3. At an upcoming meeting, ask your team to brainstorm a list of expectations that you all should adhere too. This is a great way to encourage feedback and ownership from your team.

[13]

BE THE COACH

"A champion is simply someone who did
not give up when they wanted to."

—Tom Landry, NFL coach with 20 consecutive winning
seasons, 19 NFL playoff appearances, 13 division titles,
five Super Bowl appearances, and two Super Bowl
victories.

As we've discussed, the third of the 3Ps, Performance
Accountability, deals with many of the traditional
accountability ideas: hitting business targets, following
rules (which are enforced expectations), and disciplining
when needed. But the 3Ps approach isn't grounded in
discipline. It's really about coaching your employees.

According to Tom Landry, one of the top NFL coaches
in history, coaching is supporting your players and pushing

them to stick with it when things get hard. It's about teaching them. Throughout this book I've used sporting stories, in part because I love sports and this is my book, so I get to choose the analogies we use! But I also use these examples because there are a lot of commonalities between sports and business. No matter how exceptional an athlete is, they need a coach to help them improve. The same is true of employees. No matter how they're currently performing, it's a coach, not a manager, that will take them to the next level.

Daniel Osuna was one of my assistant managers early on at Sleep Train, when I was a real Hernazi. He's now a great friend and coworker of over a decade. Daniel leads as if Dale, the company's founder, was standing next to him. When he's on the phone with guests or employees, he acts like Dale is listening in. Daniel coaches his leaders with this same idea. When they bring a challenging situation to him, he asks, "So, what would you do if you were the owner of the company? What if your name was on the outside of the building?" He coaches leaders to take an owner's level of accountability to everything they do.

Like Daniel, I'm a coach to my team members. Years ago, I started being very open about this coaching attitude and would tell new employees about it when they started. We'll talk more about onboarding in the next chapter, but first, we must get the attitude towards new and existing employees right. We need to embrace the mindset of a coach focused on making people successful—which is not the same as making people happy.

Coaching For Success, Not Happiness

Imagine I'm your personal trainer. This takes a lot of imagination, as I don't quite have the buffed muscles required for the job. But imagine you've hired me to help you lose weight, and let's pretend I know what I'm doing. I'll wake you up early for a pre-work run. I'll tell you what to eat. I'll give you a hard time when you break into the kids' leftover Halloween candy, and I'll make you do "just one more" than you want in every weights session. You might not like me, you might curse my name when your legs ache at night, but you'll achieve your goal. You'll lose weight and feel really good for it.

This morning, I told my son to empty the dishwasher. He said he was done, but he hadn't put away any of the silverware. He asked if I'd do it. "What do you think my answer will be?" I asked. He said, "You're gonna say no because you want to teach me a lesson." My son knows me well. As I watched him put away the knives and forks, I told him he'd thank me one day because I was teaching him to finish a job. I sure wasn't making him happy, but I hope I'm teaching him to be successful.

Coaching Provides Exponential Results

As any personal trainer will tell you, it's never just about losing weight. It's about the impact losing weight will have on your life; being able to keep up with your kids running around the park, feeling more comfortable in clothes that don't dig in. Unloading the dishwasher is not about the silverware; it's about the lessons you teach on finishing a job. The same is true with coaching your team at work.

Remember Jim, a Sleep Train employee of mine I mentioned earlier? He was passed over for promotion because, despite being excellent at his job, his drinking and social behavior ensured he wouldn't be respected as a leader. As a leader—a coach—it's sometimes hard to see the impact of your words in the moment, but the coaching is always more than it seems. Jim gave me an amazing opportunity to understand this when he wrote me the following letter a few years ago.

Hernani,

The other night I was leaving the ballpark and had a young man approach me that I didn't recognize right away. After a brief introduction, I remembered exactly who he was. I had coached Mike in baseball about three years ago when I was helping a local high school coach with his summer program. Mike had been reflecting on where his life changed and pivoted. This 10-minute conversation really got me thinking and kept me up late that night. I wanted to share it with you.

At the time I coached Mike, he was 14 and going through a tumultuous time in his life, yet hid it very well. His parents had long since split up, and he was starting to dabble with drugs. He didn't have a man to look up to in his life. No uncles, cousins, dad, no one. All he had were coaches to drive him and help make him a better ball player. All of this as going on behind the scenes, and I was not aware of it.

Day to day, I would push Mike, demand more, and let him know I expected more from him. I pushed him towards his breaking point but never too far. Evidently, he remembered the conversations we would have as we would drag and prep the field after practices. He remembered me telling him about the opportunities he had, that I believed in him, and how I wouldn't respect him if he didn't take advantage of his God-given abilities.

Unbeknown to me, after my summer with Mike, he went on to have a great high school career, and now has three D-1 college scholarship offers to choose from. He has life by the horns right now, and I had no idea I had an impact on his life. He wanted to find me before he left for college and let me know.

This got me thinking about thanking the people in my life that have had an impact far greater than they will ever know.

Five years ago, I was in a dark place. I wasn't happy with myself, wasn't proud of who I had become, and wasn't someone I would point out for my kids to look up to. My marriage was on the rocks, my career was not going how I would like it, my health was in shambles, and my relationship with my mom was strained. I knew I had a problem with alcohol but kept lying and telling myself I drank like most "normal" guys.

The only one that had the guts to tell me otherwise was you. You were the one that told me when everyone else was having fun, I "always seemed to be having a little more fun than everyone else." I laughed and knew it was true, but still wanted to believe it was ok. I chewed on it for a couple of years before deciding to change my life.

Looking back over the last four years of my life sober, I couldn't be more grateful for what I have, who I am, and where I have come from. I couldn't have done this by myself and take no credit for it. I am grateful that you got the wheels turning in my head and made it hard to sleep. My marriage is strong, my relationship with my mom is rock solid, and I am happier with my career than I have ever been.

Sometimes we don't realize the impact we have on others. I didn't. I thought I was just trying to help a kid. I am sure you were just being honest with me when I asked you what I could do to better my chances of a promotion. Little did you know you made a family better, and a man healthy and happy again.

Thank you,
Jim

After that conversation—the one where I talked about him having more fun than others—Jim went on to become director of sales, responsible for over two thousand employees. It wasn't just his relationships with his kids, wife, and mom that improved. The company benefitted beyond measure from Jim's new approach to life.

He says he can take no credit for his transformation, but I disagree. Jim did something incredibly difficult: he took control of an addiction. He's right, though, that no one is an island. We all need people around who will hold us accountable. That's what our conversation was. I held Jim accountable for his social behavior with tough love.

Through that, I played a part in improving his life and work performance.

Having an Impact

It means so much to me that I was able to impact the life of a good man who was in a bad place. I'm also grateful that Jim took a moment to tell me what that conversation meant to him. His openness helped me understand the power of accountability and contributed to the program you're now learning.

Steve Jobs, the founder of Apple, said, "My job is not to be easy on people. My job is to take these great people we have and to push and make them even better." That's coaching. It's not letting your would-be champions give up when things are hard, like Tom Landry said at the beginning of this chapter. Jim was profoundly impacted by being held accountable. If you use accountability to coach your team, you can have a similarly positive impact. It's powerful stuff.

♥ Take Action

1. List out any poor behaviors you've witnessed and didn't speak up about.

2. Think about coaches you've had in your life. This could be in formal settings, like Jim coaching Mike in baseball, or informally when a friend gave you advice or held you accountable, and it can be from any time. Write down what happened. How did they coach you? How did you respond? Do you see any patterns?

3. Do you currently have a coach or mentor who will hold you accountable? If not, go and ask a leader you admire if they'll be your mentor. You'll make their day, and you'll greatly benefit from their coaching.

[14]

FIRST IMPRESSIONS, ONE CHANCE

"Approximately seventy percent of new hires decide whether to stay or leave an organization within the first six months of joining."

—Human Capital Institute, an educational institution for human resource teams, talent management leaders, and business executives.

In college, I studied International Business. As part of the degree, I had to take an elective course and wanted to do psychology. Unfortunately, I waited until the last minute to sign up, and there weren't any seats left in

Psychology 101. The only kind-of-related subject still available was sociology, so that's what I took.

In one of the first lectures, the professor, Dr. Richardson, talked about what makes families dysfunctional. I was still young but knew I wanted a family. I'd never thought of a family as a social group before. Dr. Richardson said that traditionally a family starts with a man and woman dating, creating a strong bond, and eventually having a child together.

At that point, they go from being one hundred percent husband and wife to being Mom and Dad. A couple of years later they might have another child, and by now they've forgotten the bond of husband and wife. They're not having date nights. They're not connected like they were when they dated. They're just in mom and dad mode.

Without a strong connection to each other, they subconsciously reach out to form a bond with someone else. Before you know it, Mom is close to one child, and Dad the other. The parents successfully build bonds with their children, but not equally, and they forget to protect the original bond between them. Mom starts making decisions on her own, and so does Dad. One kid gets away with more, and the other resents them. Everyone acts like they're alone.

Dr. Richardson explained that when teenagers don't feel bonded to either parent, they look for connection in other places: gangs, the "wrong crowd," much-older boyfriends. Have you seen this play out anywhere?

Families are social groups, and so are workplaces. Of course, many of the dynamics are different; business leaders don't usually tell employees to tidy their rooms or be home by midnight. There are similarities, though.

When a new employee arrives, leaders must build a strong relationship with that person while maintaining their bonds with existing team members—just like when a second child is born. Leaders must have strong relationships with their fellow leaders as well as their new and old employees.

Onboarding is your chance to kick-start that bond. It's a fresh slate in which you can create a positive experience, set the right expectations, and establish yourself as a coach. It doesn't matter whether this person is new to the company or transferring from within. Effective onboarding will set you both up for success.

Onboarding Done Wrong

Unfortunately, most companies have ineffective onboarding procedures. Sometimes they're drowning and "don't have time" to train the newcomer, so they just throw them in the deep end. More often, the new recruit gets some quick, on-the-job training from an overworked, frazzled colleague, or is sat in a corner to read a fifty-page welcome manual on their own.

This usually ends with the new employee feeling overwhelmed, confused about what's expected, and disheartened. When they do get to the real work, they're not excited and definitely not productive.

This careless approach to onboarding affects turnover, too. Seventy percent of new hires decide whether to stay or leave an organization within the first six months of joining, so effective onboarding is the key to reducing turnover, as well as increasing productivity.

In case you haven't already felt the impact of high turnover, think about this: Forbes says, "Off-the-shelf estimates are available, which might set the cost of an entry-level position turning over at 50 percent of salary; mid-level at 125 percent of salary; and senior executive over 200 percent of salary." Deloitte suggests that hiring costs combined with lost productivity means each departing employee costs an average of $121,000.

To avoid these costs—financial and otherwise—leaders need to set the right expectations during onboarding, so employees have positive experiences, know what they must do to be successful, and become willing to walk through walls for their new company. We've already discussed the power of setting expectations, but let's look at how to actually do this with a new recruit.

The New Employee One-on-One

This process is for new employees, whether they've just joined the company or are transferring from within. On their first day, you must invest some time meeting with them one-on-one. I know you're busy, but reading this chapter is your only prep work for this meeting, as they will do the rest. In my experience, new employee one-on-one meetings take about two hours, and you can do them over a long lunch. This small time investment will set the groundwork for a big return in loyalty, longevity, and productivity.

Here's how to conduct a new employee one-on-one meeting:

Assign pre-work

Pre-work for this meeting is a simple one-page sheet with five questions. It's a small enough assignment that you can ask your new recruit to complete it before their first day or, if time permits, they can fill out the form immediately before your meeting.

The five questions are:

1. *Tell me about yourself. What do you love to do outside of work?*

This broad question can be really informative. Learning about extra-curricular activities will help you create positive experiences for them.

2. *Tell me about one of your favorite vacations. What was the experience like?*

This will give you clues to understand their values. Do they enjoy a peaceful atmosphere, or being surrounded by laughter, or trying something new and out-of-the-box?

3. *What would you like to learn about this company?*

If you can help them learn something they're already curious about, you'll create an instant, small win which, in turn, will generate momentum for more wins.

4. *What's your favorite communication style? Do you prefer to speak in person, over the phone, via emails, text messages, or in another way?*

Research shows that one-on-one communication is most effective, but everyone has their own preferences.

5. *How can I be the best leader for you?*

This positions you as being there to serve them and acts as a great introduction to the idea of you as the coach. You may even be pleasantly surprised to hear the new employee say something like, "Hold me accountable and give me feedback on how I can perform at my best."

Take the new hire out

There's something about leaving the office, store, job site, or wherever you usually work. A change of atmosphere makes conversations feel lighter and easier, so take your new employee out for lunch, to a coffee house, or a bench in the park. They'll be blown away that they're getting one-on-one time with their new leader.

Blowing them away with a new experience is all part of the package. I once gave a talk at Stanford University to a group of young summer camp counselors. They were training for their upcoming camp, which would have new waves of students arriving every week.

The experienced counselors told me that, after a few weeks, it's easy to forget what it's like for a student coming in fresh. But every week it's the first day of camp for the new students, and you can't cheat them out of that experience.

Disney does a great job of this. Their employees have seen the Magic Kingdom parade hundreds of times, but they never forget it's the first time these particular kids are seeing the castle and meeting Mickey Mouse. They make sure all those firsts are magical. Your workplace might not be a fairyland, but if you make your employees' first experiences magical, they will be wowed and will be ready to mirror your efforts.

Scheduling this time out also removes the temptation to set expectations in less-than-ideal ways, like over email or in a document. Remember when we talked about the best forms of communication way back in chapter six? One-on-one, in-person conversations are the most productive. At this early stage in your relationship, you and your new employee need all the benefits of this communication method. If you really can't meet in person, get on a video call.

Before you even start the formal part of the meeting, pay attention to your new employee. Take note of what beverage they order or how they take their coffee. Don't rely on your memory, here. Your big brain processes a lot of information every day, so take literal notes. Write down their partner's name, favorite football team, next vacation destination, or anything personal they mention. In the future, you'll be able to show them love by getting their favorite grande, iced, sugar-free, vanilla soy latte just right.

Review the pre-work

Ask your new team member to talk you through their pre-work answers. This will mean they're doing most of the talking. In this world, it's rare that someone is given the time and space to speak and be heard. Your simple act of listening and taking notes will start to win their heart.

You'll spend about eighty percent of your time on this part of the process, so there's no need to rush. Ask questions and take notes. Both these actions demonstrate you're paying attention. They show you care about what your employee is saying, and therefore about them.

If they talk you through all their answers and you still have plenty of time left, go back and ask more about their activities or the vacation they loved. It might feel like you're just chatting, but you're actually developing an essential bond, and their answers will give you clues on how they like to be treated and what they care about.

Set expectations and establish yourself as the coach

In the last twenty percent of your time, you'll talk about expectations and your role as their coach. An easy way into this conversation is to ask if there's a leadership model they live by. This will reveal any early learnings they have and give you an "in" to talk about your way of doing things.

Tell them you'll be on time every day and expect them to be, too. Talk about not using your phone during meetings, or whatever expectations you have. Explain how you like to receive the gift of feedback.

This is where you'll explain the concept of being a coach, and doing everything in your power to make them successful (which, as we've said, is different from happy). Then get into balanced accountability, catching people doing things right, and that you expect them to hold themselves, their colleagues, and even you accountable.

Encourage them to make decisions by confiding your trust. Say you want them to be bold in business and steal second base. Give them permission to make decisions, so long as they're caring for the company.

Be open about the bond you're developing with this meeting. Tell them you read something in a book (ahem) about the sociology of family bonds, and how it's mirrored in workplace teams. Discuss building a bond with them, and maintaining the ties with your existing team members, so you're all on the same page. You can admit you won't always agree on everything but, with these bonds, you'll always agree on where you're headed.

Ask extra questions

End your one-on-one by asking if there are any ideas they feel you need to implement right away. More senior executives respond best to this question, but it's worth asking everyone as there might be a quick win you can work on to create a positive experience.

Even if their idea is difficult to implement, or if they have no suggestions yet, this question shows you're a proactive leader interested in their input. Sometimes it gives you the opportunity to explain why things are done a certain way.

As you create and maintain a bond with your new employee, you'll find they will want to follow you. I don't mean this in a weird, stalker way. I mean they'll happily follow you to every new goal, sales target, or workplace ambition. You'll win their heart.

You might think this is easy to do when you're starting fresh with a new employee and, to an extent, you're right. If you can resist the temptation to throw them in the deep end and take time to build a bond, it's not hard. You might even enjoy getting out of the workplace and learning more about your new employees. In the next chapter, we'll talk about the challenge of building or repairing bonds with your existing team members. You should know that can be fun, too!

♥ Take Action

1. What have onboarding issues cost you in the past? Consider the lost production, time, and money involved in hiring a new employee and bringing them up to the same level as the employee who left.

2. How will you integrate this new onboarding process?

3. Set a Calendar reminder for 90 and 180 days from when you first met with the employee to follow up. They will be impressed that you followed through.

[15]

CREATING THE DREAM TEAM

"None of us is as smart as all of us."

—Ken Blanchard, management expert and author of over sixty books, including *The One Minute Manager*, *Raving Fans*, and *Whale Done!*

In the last chapter, we discussed effectively setting expectations with new team members. It's important to do the same with your existing employees. Permitting and therefore promoting poor behavior is passive leadership, but there are active ways to set expectations, so your staff becomes the ultimate dream team.

Coaches (in the traditional sense) are great at setting expectations. A football team knows they are expected to win games. How do they know if they're winning? That's easy. They check the scoreboard. If it shows they have a higher score than their opponent, they know they're in the lead. The scoreboard also has a clock, showing how much time remains, so players know how long they have until the final whistle.

How does your team know they're winning at work? How do you keep score? Do your players know how much time is left to win the game? Part of setting expectations is ensuring everyone knows the game you're playing, how you're keeping score, and the time frame you have to win. SMART goals are an excellent way to do this. You've likely heard of SMART goals before; they're targets which are:

Specific—they can be succinctly described;

Measurable—there are numbers attached;

Achievable—they are realistic;

Relevant—they are focused on a result which is related to the team's purpose; and

Time-bound—there is a deadline by which the goal should be achieved.

What Do SMART Goals Look Like?

Imagine you understand that feedback is a gift and you know winning the hearts of your employees is key to improving performance. You want input from your employees on how they feel about the company, so you work towards winning their hearts. To capture feedback, you create an engagement survey—a set of questions to be answered anonymously, which will gauge employees' engagement with their team and the company as a whole.

You send out the survey for the first time and get a baseline average score.

You then set a SMART goal to improve your average score by five percent in the next survey, which will take place in six months. The goal is specific; it's extremely clear. The percentage points make it measurable. You might eventually want a twenty percent improvement, but you've chosen five percent for now because it's achievable. The goal is relevant as it'll push you closer towards the result of a highly-engaged staff. The six-month deadline makes the goal time-bound.

SMART goals are often based on Key Performance Indicators (KPIs). KPIs are measurable values that demonstrate how well a company is performing. In the example above, the survey scores would be considered a KPI if the company was focused on improving employee engagement. You might have KPIs you monitor in your role as leader. These can be a great starting point for team or individual employee goal-setting.

Keeping Score

Whether you're tracking KPIs or anything else, goals need a scoreboard. You and your employees need to be able to track how they're performing. For team goals, the scoreboard must be in public view.

When every team member can see how they rank compared to their colleagues, two things happen. First, the top performers get a boost from seeing their name on top. They get all the benefits we talked about in chapter eleven when we discussed magnifying small wins. Second, the bottom performers will up their game. Public scoreboards drive results.

With team goals, you usually see a few employees rise to the challenge, and some dig their heels in and resist. There could be a few reasons you have resistors on your team. They might believe the goal is unachievable or irrelevant. If you haven't properly been through P1: Personal Accountability they may not respect you enough yet to jump on board. You might be dealing with an energy vampire (which we'll discuss more in the next chapter).

If you can't see and address a clear reason for resistors digging in their heels, let nature take its course. As time goes on and progress (or a lack of it) is publicly displayed, they will see you celebrating those who do well. Don't point out the resistors' poor performance, but magnify the small wins along the way of those who are successful. The resistors will notice. They'll know everyone else can see them in last place. In time, they'll jump on the bandwagon.

If that time is ticking by too slow, make a personal check-in with your bottom performers. In person is best. If that's not possible, a video call is the next best option, followed by a phone call. Schedule a meeting in advance and take them out of the workplace, so they're not embarrassed in front of their colleagues. Say that you've noticed they're struggling with this particular goal, and ask what you can do to help. Use phrases like "below average" and "holding the team back." No one wants to be below the line or the team's weak link. Encourage them to come up with a solution; they'll engage with it more if it comes from them.

You'll quickly discover how proactive they are and get a sense of whether they're willing to up their game. If they're not, then maybe you don't want them on your team. It's more likely, though, that they'll appreciate being held accountable and rise to the challenge. Who knows... they may, in time, turn into your top team member!

One last note here: If even your top performers aren't making progress fast enough, don't criticize them. They're your top influencers, and they set the vibe. If they feel unappreciated, that negativity will spread to everyone else. As long as things are moving in the right direction, continue to praise your top performers. Then reevaluate your goals to see if they're realistically achievable in the time frame you've provided.

Individual Goals

Use the Personal Review Report Card we discussed in chapter eight to set individual goals with your team members. If you need a reminder, this is a one-page document your employees complete every six months in preparation for one-on-one feedback meetings with you. Employees love getting feedback in those meetings, and the report card makes it really easy for leaders to manage them.

There are only six questions on the report card, and the last one asks employees to list two work-related goals and one personal goal. This is the perfect place to set expectations through goal-setting. Return to the more detailed advice in chapter eight, download the report card from BalancedIQ.com, guide your employees to ensure their goals are SMART, and enjoy watching them exceed their own expectations.

Successful Screw-Ups

Achieving individual or team goals doesn't need to be all-or-nothing. Ideally, all your employees would exceed all their goals, but you can still have success if they don't quite get there. A former colleague of mine, Matt Anderson, calls this the "successful screw-up."

Matt and I worked closely together to create the University of Sleep Train, a six-week training course to turn average sales employees into sales professionals. We worked so closely together, in fact, that my wife Angie referred to Matt as my work wife.

Matt and I were both very proactive at work. We'd do whatever we thought was good for the business, and ask for forgiveness later. Sometimes that got us into trouble, and we'd have to take the hit, but that attitude gave us a lot of success together.

One of our proactive adventures turned into a successful screw-up. We were trying to reduce exchange rates on box springs. We sold two types of box springs: tall and low profile. It was common for a customer to order the tall box spring, get it delivered, then exchange it for the low profile version after seeing how huge the tall one was. Yes, they'd already seen it in the big, spacious store, but in their cozy bedroom, that tall box spring suddenly felt enormous.

Matt and I thought the solution was simple. We just needed to display all the in-store tall mattresses on low profile box springs, and customers would buy what they saw. We were wrong. Customers saw these low-looking mattresses and decided they wanted something higher.

We ended up with more people ordering tall box springs, and they all had the same problem when seeing it at home. Exchange rates increased. Our simple, proactive solution turned into a giant screw-up.

At the risk of driving our store staff crazy, we switched all the box springs back to tall ones and rolled out new processes. Customers would now go home with a paper tape measure, which they'd use to measure their bed frame. Then the customer would call and confirm which box spring they needed.

It worked! There was a tiny bit more work for the customer, but it gave them a much better result. They only had to stay home for one delivery, not two, and they didn't have the hassle of arranging a return. For the company, we added the minor cost of paper tape measures, and massively reduced expenses around exchanges. Our amazing store staff forgave us for all the box spring back-and-forth, and everyone was happy.

It was only thanks to the initial screw-up that we learned what was necessary to be successful. Dale, our CEO, didn't punish us for taking a chance, as he encouraged us to take risks to make improvements. When your team understands that screw-ups can lead to successes, they will be more comfortable being assertive, trying new things, possibly failing, and finding success through it.

When our exchange rate increased after the first switch-up, Matt and I were hauled in front of our leaders to explain. Matt was brilliant and didn't hold back; he confidently declared it a successful screw-up because we now knew more than before, and would be able to fix the problem. Sure, it would take longer than if we'd reduced the exchange rate immediately, but challenges are just that: challenging.

An initial fail doesn't mean you've failed for good; it means you're more informed for the next step. Our leaders gave us a proverbial high-five for being proactive, asked how we planned to fix the increased exchange rate, and took note of what we'd learned for future use. Even at that stage, Matt considered it a successful screw-up, and once exchange rates were drastically reduced, no one argued with him.

A very successful screw-up lesson with this scenario was learning first to screw-up small. We started the process of pilot testing new ideas before the company wide launches. From this date forward, we used test and control groups. This allowed us to make small screw-ups first, before launching the initiative company wide.

Four Fs to Encourage Successful Screw-ups

To successfully screw-up, every one of your team members must know they are safe to be assertive in achieving their goals. I recommend sharing the following statements with your team.

1. *Fail Small & Only Make the Same Mistake Once*
2. *Focus Resolving, Not Quitting.*
3. *Find Resources to Fix Mistakes*
4. *Finally Celebrate Screw-Ups*

♥ Take Action

1. What behaviors have you permitted and promoted in the past? What was the result?

2. Create a SMART goal template. Use it to set your team's SMART goals and KPIs. Decide how you will use a public scoreboard for team goals.

3. Tell your team members you're happy for them to have successful screw-ups. Download the free successful screw-up poster from BalancedIQ.com and share it with them.

[16]

THE UNFORGIVABLES

"It is not only what we do, but also what we do not do, for which we are accountable."

—Molière, actor and poet, widely regarded as one of the greatest writers in universal literature.

Molière was right; each individual is accountable for his or her actions and lack of action. As a leader, it's up to you to hold your team members accountable. As we've discussed, we do this through coaching, second chances, goal-setting, and leading with love. That is hands-down the best way to deal with challenging performance-related behaviors.

However, we all know some workplace actions must be addressed in less squishy terms. I'm talking about the unforgivable stuff, the fireable offenses, the things that make lawyers twitchy and leaders want to hide. To be an effective leader with a high-performing team, you must know how to handle gross misconduct behaviors.

Gross Misconduct

Does your team know what actions are considered unforgivable at your workplace? Don't assume they know what counts as a fireable offense, no matter how obvious it seems to you. Remember: you must set clear expectations for team members. That's true for big, behavioral issues as much as performance-related ones.

Gross misconduct is the term generally used for any behaviors that result in immediate termination. They can also be referred to as code of ethics violations. If you're unclear what's considered gross misconduct in your workplace, schedule time to talk with someone from your human resources (HR) department. If you don't have an HR department, ask your own leader.

Below is a list of actions that commonly come under the umbrella of gross misconduct. Thanks to Sleep Train for providing this example.

- Workplace or associate-instigated violence, or related threats;
- Disruptive behavior, including abusive or vulgar language;
- Any use, possession, or distribution of alcohol or illegal substance on duty or on company premises and/or reporting to work under the influence of such a substance;

- Sexual, physical, or verbal harassment or abuse, including harassment or abuse that is targeted towards a member of a protected class as defined in Title VII (race or color, national origin, sex or gender, religion, age, and disability);
- Repeated safety violations;
- Bringing firearms, explosives, knives, or other weapons onto company property;
- Inappropriate use of the internet, telephone, or email, for example, to access pornography;
- Criminal damage to company property;
- Unauthorized possession or removal of company property or assets;
- Serious insubordination;
- Fraud of any kind;
- Failure of, or refusal to submit to, a drug test;
- Violations of federal, state, or local law; or
- Exposure of confidential company information to unauthorized persons.

Tips for Dealing with Gross Misconduct Behaviors

1. Don't avoid it

A lot of leaders avoid conversations about gross misconduct. If you've been putting off a serious discussion, you're not alone. Sometimes leaders play out the conversation in their mind, see how awkward it will be, and build up a mental block around the whole thing. Usually, though, the real talk goes much smoother than the imagined one.

Severe situations are best handled immediately and in private. Ask your employee, "Do you have a moment?" and take them into your office or a separate area. If you didn't handle it immediately, it's not too late. Arrange a conversation with the employee in question as soon as possible—even if you don't know all the facts or feel unsure.

2. Set it up right

Minor situations can be handled one-on-one, but when discussing gross misconduct behaviors, you should have a witness present. The witness should be a superior or someone from HR, but not the employee's teammate. That's embarrassing for them, and you want to handle this respectfully. Regardless of the situation's severity, you can always bring in a witness if you feel the employee is a bully or might get physical.

Sit next to the employee, not across from them. This creates a less confrontational atmosphere, which will help the employee engage in conversation. You want a casual, non-threatening conversation. You will get a more accurate understanding of what's happened if you get them talking and really listen.

3. Ask questions

I used to go into these meetings with a defensive attitude. I felt like I'd been attacked. In time, I learned that I got better results when I understood where the employee was coming from, even if they were in the wrong.

To get their side of the story, you need to ask questions. In sports, the referee sometimes misses an initial foul. They only catch the retaliation. Asking questions will help you discover if another employee provoked them, or if there's anything else you should know.

"Tell me more," is an excellent phrase to use here. "What's your side of the story?" can also get a good response.

4. Focus on facts

Talk about facts. Opinions are subjective and can be shot down. Short, specific fact statements keep things straightforward. You might say, "On this date, you did this.... Tell me more about that."

You should be able to focus on two or three specific facts. If you have pages of stuff to discuss, you probably haven't been doing your job as a leader. You haven't dealt with issues head on, and have let them build up. Choose a few of the most significant or most recent issues, and focus on them.

5. Be clear about the future

If you need more time to get the bottom of a situation or figure out your next move, be open about that. Don't feel pressured to make a decision on the spot. Tell the employee you want to treat them fairly, and need some time to figure out what that looks like. Confirm when they will hear from you next.

If it's not appropriate for the employee to return to their regular work, give them a time out. This can take many forms: You can send them home for the day, ask them to work in a different environment (like another store, office area, or part of the job site), or put them on a formal suspension. Use the time out to meet with any other individuals involved, and get advice from HR.

HR Guides, You Lead

HR is there to guide you. They will provide advice, but it must be you who leads the situation. Punting it over the HR and letting them deal with it will hold you back as a leader. Just as parents can't pass the buck when things get tough, neither can you. You must be the one to handle crucial decisions and conversations. You will become a better leader, and your team will respect you more for it.

Transformational Suspensions

Suspensions are a useful tool when it will take longer than a few hours to investigate the situation. It's an extended time out that gives everyone some breathing room while you figure out what to do.

When you send an employee home:

Clarify if they will be paid. (Rules vary by area so your HR department will confirm this for you.)

Set a time frame for the suspension—as short as possible while allowing enough time to investigate.

Confirm they should not work from home, online, or in any other manner during this time.

Have them commit to not speaking to anyone from the company, or retaliating in any way.

In my experience, a suspension rarely ends with a dismissal. Usually, it acts as disciplinary action on its own—a reality check that holds the employee accountable for their behavior. It scares them, and they return a different person.

This happened with Mike, one of our warehouse managers. Mike contacted Tracy, our HR leader, about an employee that made a mistake. When Mike confronted the employee, he owned up to making a mistake and acknowledging that he had been warned before.

Mike then said to Tracy, "See, now I feel like since he's confirmed that I've spoken to him about this before, I have to terminate him." Tracy responded, "Well, you can, or you can also do something just short of letting him go and let him know that you did this because he told you the truth. But, had he lied and not told you the truth, we would have terminated him."

Mike felt great about this option, and we decided to suspend him for a few days with a final warning. We knew the word would get out to others that employees should own up to their faults because the penalty for lying would be much bigger.

The employee went on to become a very high performer for the company. He moved up the ranks and led fantastic teams. He made a mistake, was suspended, and returned more committed and better-performing than ever before.

The Risk of Wrongful Suspensions

You might worry about suspending someone who turns out to be innocent. It's a fair concern. In more than twenty years of leadership, this has happened to me twice. I suspended someone, investigated the incident, and discovered they did nothing wrong.

In both those cases, I called the employee, told them my findings, admitted I shouldn't have suspended them, and invited them back. Both employees returned, and we continued long and productive working relationships.

Salaried employees are usually paid while suspended, but for an hourly-paid employee who was wrongly suspended, take the hit and pay them their average workday.

Suspending an innocent employee is a small risk which can be easily fixed with an acknowledgment, an apology, and a paycheck. The bigger risk is in not properly addressing issues as they come up. That will destroy your team, because you'll be permitting, and therefore promoting, destructive behavior.

Promoting an Employee to Customer

Sometimes a suspension is not enough. It might be that an initial offense was so grave that you cannot keep the team member in your employment, or it could be following multiple smaller misconducts. I've fired a lot of people in my career. It is always tough, and it's always worthwhile— for you, your team, and the individual themselves.

When you suspect you'll have to fire someone, talk to HR before doing anything else. It's best to be upfront with HR, but if it's a sensitive issue, you can talk it out without naming names. Ask what they'd recommend in a "hypothetical situation," if you must.

Every country and state has different laws regarding dismissals, and a good HR professional will know the laws that relate to your situation. Even if this conversation feels difficult, you must talk to HR. As a manager who is aware of a major infraction, you are putting the company and yourself at huge legal risk if you don't. Speaking up does not make you a snitch; it means you are a responsible, professional leader who must answer to the law.

Your HR department will have guidelines for how to talk to the employee in question, who should be present, and what paperwork should be completed. Follow these exactly.

As you go through the process, it might be helpful to consider that you are promoting the employee to a customer. As much as they may want this job, something is not right, and, in the long run, they'll be happier as a customer. It will allow them to reflect on what they did wrong and how they can prevent this at their next job.

In the book *Lead with LUV: A Different Way to Create Real Success*, the authors tell a story they heard from Herb Kelleher, the founder of Southwest Airlines. Herb spoke about a woman, Mrs. Crabapple, who frequently flew on Southwest, and was constantly disappointed with every aspect of the company's operation. She became known as "The Pen Pal" because, after every flight, she wrote in with a complaint. Her last letter recited a litany of complaints and momentarily stumped Southwest's customer relations people. They asked for Herb's help, and forwarded him Mrs. Crabapple's email. Within sixty seconds, Herb replied with the following: Dear Mrs. Crabapple, We will miss you. Love, Herb.

Energy Vampires

There's one last type of employee behavior I want you to consider unforgivable: unrepentant energy sucking. I call team members who engage in this energy vampires. You might think of them as negative nellies, rain clouds, or a pain in the you-know-what.

Whatever choice words you use, I bet you know this behavior. Energy vampires are nothing but hard work. They don't just challenge your ideas... they straight up shoot them to pieces without offering any suggestions for improvements. They're the first to say, "I told you so" when the team's efforts don't work out. They're probably not your top performers, yet somehow they demand a disproportionate amount of attention. There's always something going on with them.

I'm not suggesting sucking up energy is on par with the gross misconduct behaviors mentioned above. Of course, harassment and safety violations are more severe. However, it's amazing how often leaders let this energy stuff slide, ending up drained with nothing left to give the rest of their team.

You might think that's okay, and that the rest of the team doesn't need you as the energy vampires do. But can you imagine how much better your entire department would perform if you didn't surrender emotional and mental energy to that one low-performing person?

Don't give in to the drama and let energy vampires suck up all you have to give. Do not let them dictate how you spend your valuable energy. You are not at their mercy. You control your energy.

One bad player on the football field means the team won't win and, as the coach, you need to sub them out. That could mean a short time out for a pep talk, a longer stint on the sidelines while doing extra training, or even booting them off the team for good.

Address the vampire in the room. Take them aside and have a serious conversation. Tell them they're sucking up a disproportionate percentage of your energy. Use the tips from this chapter for difficult conversations, and announce you will no longer permit this behavior.

Clearly confirm what you expect of them moving forward, and put it in writing. Then share the conversation and the written report with your human resources department. Monitor the employee's change—or lack of it—and have a follow-up meeting within thirty, sixty, and ninety days to discuss progress. If there is no progress, consider if it's time to replace this player for good.

Hakuna Matata

I'm a little embarrassed to admit this, but my favorite movie is *The Lion King*. Yes, the animated Disney movie. I'd love to say it's something cool like *The Godfather* or *Die Hard*, but there's something about the grit of that little lion cub that just gets me.

One of the most famous phrases from that movie is "hakuna matata." As the accompanying song says, it means "no worries" in Swahili, an eastern African language. Hakuna matata has become my mantra. I repeat it several times a day. When I feel energy vampires coming close, demanding their problems take priority, I think hakuna matata. After a difficult gross misconduct conversation, I repeat this little phrase to myself. When I'm disappointed in someone else's behavior, I use it to remember this isn't the end of the world.

There are bigger things to worry about—setting my kids up for success, making sure my wife knows I love her, keeping a roof over our heads and food in our bellies. Work is important. It fulfills me in a way nothing else does. I suspect the same is true for you.

But when things are challenging? Hakuna matata. Even—or rather, especially—when things don't feel carefree, try repeating this phrase. See how it impacts you. If it helps put things in perspective, great. If it doesn't serve you, then no worries!

Whether you quote The Lion King to yourself or use something more sophisticated, the key is to address unforgivable behaviors, then get yourself back into a headspace that will help you and your team become greater than ever before. That's what we'll focus on in the next chapter.

♥ Take Action

1. Have you permitted any unforgivable behaviors?

2. Are there any unforgivable behaviors currently in your workplace? If so, talk to your HR department about them at the earliest opportunity.

3. Write down your top Energy Vampire and list facts (not opinions) on why they suck the energy out of the team. Then meet with your HR department to discuss on a plan to address them with the person directly.

[17]

GREATER THAN THEMSELVES

"The greatest leaders make others greater than themselves."

—Steve Farber, founder of Extreme Leadership, Inc and author of bestselling book *Greater Than Yourself.*

When my wife, Angie, went into labor with our daughter, we felt the same anxious excitement as all soon-to-be-parents. With the first contraction, we packed up our bags, the car seat, the stroller, a super-special teddy bear, soothers, bottles, and the kitchen sink, and raced off to the hospital. I was frantic, so I dropped Angie at the hospital doors and took off to park the car.

Angie went on in and filled out some paperwork. The nurse came and asked a few standard questions. She checked Angie's vitals and did a quick ultrasound. That's when everything fell apart.

She couldn't find a heartbeat. She called in the doctor, who couldn't see any sign of life, either. Just nine months earlier, we'd sat in that same hospital and listened as the ultrasound picked up Carmina's heart beating strong and steady and filling us with joy. That was when it really clicked: I was going to be a dad. Now... we thought she'd be stillborn.

Angie pushed through 12 hours of intense labor. The whole time the doctors assured us that sometimes this happens, and it works out okay, but no one knew for sure. A lot of bad thoughts ran through my mind in those long hours. Finally, it was time. Angie gave birth to our tiny little girl, and I cut the umbilical cord.

Carmina didn't cry. I could tell she was still with us, though. Then she screamed, stopped suddenly, and turned blue. The doctors tore her from my arms and started ripping things from her throat. Angie and I could do nothing but watch.

They revived Carmina, but she was very unstable. For several days we didn't know if she'd make it. That girl's a fighter, though. She's a winner. Today, she's a strong, smart, and athletic teenager. Her laugh makes me giggle.

Becoming a parent was the scariest and most life-changing experience I've had. Four years later, Angie championed through another labor and our son, Riley, joined us. Thankfully, his birth went smoothly. We call him Riley Smiley because of his huge, infectious grin. He pushes me to be a better person.

Understanding Accountability

I started to understand accountability when I was nine-years-old, and my dad forced me to do as I'd promised and milk Cow Number One. The years passed, I became an adult, and had the good fortune to fall into an amazing job. With the grace and teachings of my colleagues and mentors, I learned how to lead.

The life lessons came thick and heavy as Carmina was born, and even more so after Riley arrived. Angie and I stumbled through all those parenting decisions, and our beautiful children taught us so much. They still do every day. As they grew from babies to strong-willed toddlers, I started to appreciate that accountability is integral to love. I love my kids, so I hold them accountable for their actions, as that will help them become the best versions of themselves.

A great leader loves their team members, so holds them accountable for their actions. They respect their employees as adults, and at the same time, they bring the lessons of a loving parent to those relationships. I hope, in these pages, I've helped you do that.

We've covered a lot, and I know it can feel overwhelming, particularly if your life is busy with challenging work situations. High turnover, mediocre performance, and poorly engaged employees might tempt you to shelve these ideas until things are quieter. Please understand that the 3Ps: Personal, Positive, and Performance Accountability is what will get you to that quieter, more productive, less stressful place. I know because not only have I mentored countless other leaders through this, but I experienced it firsthand.

Making a Mark

When I first became a store manager, I was a bull-headed, unhappy Hernazi. I was doing my best for the company and working hard, yet no one wanted to work for me. Forget being loyal enough to walk through walls for me—my employees would run through walls to avoid us being in a room alone. I wasn't getting the best of them. Sales numbers were strong but unsustainable, and I was on borrowed time before losing control of my people and my store.

My mentors and colleagues helped me see the problem, and I held myself accountable to a higher standard. I became aware of my victim mentality. I stopped fixating on thoughts like, Poor me... all my employees hate me, and became more solution-oriented.

Remember five-year-old Garrett? He faced challenges far greater than anything I've experienced. He stood up to cancer and refused to let it define him. He took control of how he'd be remembered. I don't have Garrett's bravery. He was a uniquely inspirational young man. My concerns were ridiculously trivial by comparison, but my work mattered, so I did my best to adopt a Garrett-style superhero attitude.

I learned to communicate more effectively with my team in person, over email, and on social media. I checked myself—and my daughter checked me—and we found habits I could improve on. I trained myself to stop making insensitive, throwaway comments, realizing how disrespectful and destructive they are. My old district manager, Matt, taught me feedback is a gift. He helped me appreciate hearing honestly from employees, even when it's hard.

I used more positive language and saw the uplifting, ripple effect that had on my team. One word at a time, we created a more positive environment, and we actually enjoyed being in each other's presence. We snowballed this with positive experiences, and I was blown away by the incredible atmosphere that rolled into our workplace. We had more fun and were more productive. I felt lighter. As I saw the power of positivity, I held myself accountable to foster it further.

I was honored with more senior roles at Sleep Train, and worked with thousands of wonderful employees—and some challenging ones, too. They all helped me grow. Even as I was appointed president, I understood that the title wasn't important. Whatever my business card said, my real job was to be a coach.

I discovered the power of setting clear expectations with new and existing team members, and never taking for granted that they knew what was in my head or heart. I realized that being firm with unforgivable behavior was more loving than letting it slide. There were still times I had to promote an employee to customer, but I could do it with respect, so everyone—including the individual being dismissed—was better off. Having won the hearts of my employees, challenges like that were so much easier to handle.

Holding myself and my team accountable meant we could all become greater than before, both as employees and individuals. That was the mark I left on my little corner of this world, and it's what I pass on to you in these pages.

Commit to Yourself

Back in chapter one, I asked you to make a commitment to yourself. I know you want to improve as a leader—it's why you picked up this book—so I asked you to commit to reading all the way through and acting on the advice. Now, you've almost finished the book. Congratulations! We have just one chapter left which is equal parts fascinating, exciting, and devastating (you'll see).

But this book isn't the end. Acting on its advice is the beginning of your turnaround. Whatever your work situation is right now, you can start doing things differently and get different results.

Don't you owe it to yourself to try this life-changing leadership model? If things at work aren't as good as you'd like, it's time to make the change. As Steve Farber said, "The greatest leaders make others greater than themselves." With the guidelines in this book, you have the tools to do that.

You can hold yourself and others accountable to become greater. It may be uncomfortable at first, but discomfort won't kill you. It won't feel worse than that nagging feeling that says you're not doing everything you can.

The 3Ps will help you push past discomfort and create a successful team who listens, really listens, when you speak and gives insightful and encouraging feedback in meetings. They'll hit deadlines like a bullseye. Turnover will plummet and you'll start giving out trophies for years of service. You'll have a team who's openly and enthusiastically on your side, willing to do all they can for you. They'll exceed their targets, grow your business, and love working together. Can you imagine it? Now let's work for it.

♥ Take Action

1. What is your vision for your team's future? What will it take to get you there?

2. How will your workplace look like when you accomplish your vision? How ill your team feel?

3. Make a note of all the action steps you've already taken towards the 3Ps: Personal, Positive, and Performance accountability. Take a moment to appreciate your efforts. Then, write down what your next action step will be.

4. Type a letter to yourself for one year in the future, describing what your vision looks like and how you feel for achieving your vision. Include an affirmation to yourself on how important you are to your team's success.

   • When you're done, put that letter into a future calendar invite one year from today.

[18]

ACCOUNTABILITY TO GIVE BACK

"We make a living by what we get; we make a life by what we give."

—popularly attributed to Winston Churchill, former British prime minister, and Nobel Prize winner.

Many of your newer employees may be young adults diving into their first real job. Some of the young adults who have the hardest time adjusting to workplace expectations—and so benefit the most from positive accountability—are those who grew up in foster care. There are over 425,000 children in foster care in the United States, with a new child entering the system every two minutes. According to UNICEF, approximately 2.7

million children live in institutional care worldwide. Many have experienced abuse, neglect, and poverty. Some have seen their parents pass away or be imprisoned.

I was introduced to this subject by Sleep Train's founder and my former leader, Dale Carlsen, who wrote the foreword to this book. Dale is CEO and chairman of the board of the Ticket to Dream Foundation, which partners with businesses and local communities to provide school supplies, holiday gifts, properly fitting clothing and shoes, and experiences for foster children of all ages.

I want to thank you for buying this book. I'm donating a portion of your purchase price to help foster kids. Angie and I are not in a position to foster kids ourselves, but this is a small way we can support the foster community. I want to ask you to be accountable for giving back to your community—whether that's by supporting foster kids or doing something else that speaks to you.

As Dale knows more about this, I'll let him tell you how holding yourself accountable to give back can improve both your business and the world we all share.

From Dale Carlsen, CEO and Chairman of the Board for Ticket to Dream

When I first started my company, there was a radio morning show which ran a toy drive for at-risk kids in the community. The DJ for the show called and asked if they could use my trucks to deliver the toys. I said sure and offered to help with the drop-offs.

I'll never forget what I saw during those deliveries. Kids were sleeping in too small of pajamas in beds so old and worn they slumped in the middle. Some were sleeping on couches and some of these kids were in households that only had piles of clothes to sleep on. There was no way those kids were getting a good night's sleep.

I've always believed a good education is vital, and if a kid isn't getting a good night's sleep, it's hard for them to concentrate in school. Poor sleep can create or exacerbate all kinds of behavioral and emotional challenges, as well as slow cognitive processing. These were good kids who were already at a disadvantage due to the circumstances surrounding them, and the lack of sleep they were getting was just one more challenge they were up against. On top of that, we noticed that they often did not have some of their basic needs, like warm jackets or shoes that were not worn out or fit them properly.

My heart broke for these kids. I was raised in a middle class family with great parents who loved me and were there for me. These were at risk kids in my community including foster kids, who, for one reason or another, did not have parents to care for them. The foster parents that thankfully stepped in to help, often just did not have enough funds to provide for all the kids needs, due to limited government assistance.

Being raised to always give back, I was determined to make this my cause. Now, at that point in my career, I did not have any money. I did, however, have access to new, supportive mattresses and great vendors who also wanted to help, and agreed to lower my cost and even donate additional beds. We started our first giving back program and called it *Mattress 4 Kids!* The next year, when the station did their drive, we were not only able to give these kids new toys for the holidays, but Sleep Train gave them a new mattress, Payless Shoes gave them new shoes, and a local cleaner collected new jackets for each of the kids.

On another delivery round, we visited a young boy who really, really wanted a basketball. He was so excited when we gave him one. Then, he saw the mattress we were hauling in. His mouth dropped open and he ran over and jumped on the mattress and hugged it. He then asked if it was "really for him" and then screamed with excitement. He said, "A bed just for me? A bed that no one else has peed on! Thank you!"

The struggle for foster kids

In the United States, kids end up in the foster care system not because of anything they did, but because their parents have died, gone to jail, suffer from addition or just can't care for them. The kids did nothing wrong. Once in the system, they will be placed in foster homes or group homes with the hope of one day being reunited with their parents, once the parent has resolved their issues, or being taken in by a relative (kinship care), or otherwise hopefully adopted. Unfortunately, the adoption rate is way too low and many kids are left in the system until they emancipate out at 18 years of age.

We take these kids, who have often suffered abuse, neglect, been exposed to drugs and prostitution, or suffered the loss of their parents and we dump them in a system that is severely broken. On average they will be placed in at least three homes and up to as many as twenty homes before they turn 18. Then, if that's not enough, we kick them out into society, often without a job, money, or even a place to live and we tell them to go be good citizens. The resulting statistics are horrific, with 40 percent becoming homeless, 25 percent being imprisoned within two years, 70 percent of the women becoming pregnant within three years—with the cycle starting again; and 60 percent of sex trafficking victims coming from foster care.

Foster families and organizations do the best they can, but they're underfunded and lack support. The government subsidies help, but in many states, the funding covers less than half the cost of raising a child. Foster parents have to pay out of pocket to care for these kids, and most of them do this because their hearts break for them, but they struggle to pay the bills.

Understandably, new shoes, sports equipment, school supplies, jackets, holiday gifts, and even pajamas, are not always in the budget for these families. Unfortunately, the problem is that when a kid turns up at school with holes in their shoes, they become known as "that kid." When they do not have the school supplies necessary to do their homework they fall further behind (less than half graduate from high school). When it comes to extra curricular activities, like sports, music or dance lessons, scouting, and other activities that teach these young kids the skills and experience needed to succeed—such as teamwork, problem solving, achieving goals, and work ethics—there is no one to pay for these activities either. They miss out on the amazing life skills that come through participating in sports, music, the arts, and all the other activities they're left out of. They don't get to practice playing with others, strategizing, being a good team member, and working hard for success. This effectively tells them that they do not matter!

A new mattress was just one small way I could help. These mattresses had to be new, as I spent my days telling parents on the sales floor about the importance of a new, supportive mattress for the development of a young child's back. I couldn't then turn around and suggest foster kids didn't deserve the same quality as the other kids. By the end of my time with Sleep Train, we were giving away thousands of mattresses a year. Thanks to the help of my vendors, our customers, and our employees, thousands of foster kids were getting better sleep and had a little more energy to cope with challenging days.

Over the years, we expanded our involvement. We knew our brand was a trusted name in the community, so we decided to use that to promote a school supply drive, asking the public to bring pencils, backpacks, paper, etc., into our stores to donate to kids in care. By then we had branches all over the west coast, so there were plenty of drop-off spots. The public came through and donated thousands of items. We then asked for clothes, then pajamas, then shoes, then gifts for the holidays, and finally just cash to pay for those extra curricular expenses. We repeated the process, year in and year out, always separating our messaging about the drives for foster kids from our sales promotions.

It's sometimes heart-wrenching to see how much these small donations impact these kids' lives. We recently gave a pair of Superman pajamas to a seven-year-old boy.

He ran around the room shouting, "I'm a superhero! I'm a superhero! Maybe now I can help my mom." This broke my heart, but reinforced how important these little things were to these kids.

Pajamas won't cure a mom's drug habit or make her a more present parent, but for a moment that boy believed life could be better. That hope is worth something. Hope keeps people going. When there's nothing else, hope that someone out there cares can be a life raft for a lost boy.

Giving back for the right reason

You give back because it's the right thing to do, not to promote your business. I didn't want to tell someone, "Buy a bed, save a kid." That just wasn't right. I was raised that you give back because it is the right thing to do, not because it helps you. Consequently we kept our selling message completely separate from our foster kids message. None of our sales ads spoke about foster kids, and none of the promotions for school supplies drives mentioned mattresses.

When the public responded to our collection drives with such strength, it truly inspired our employees. We watched as a local girls soccer team collected and donated over three hundred coats, and saw seven- and eight-year-olds asking for shoes for foster kids in lieu of birthday presents. We watched as families would come in together to just drop off items and we saw those who themselves could not afford much bring items in for others. We were privileged to take in the clothes and shoes and other donations, and see their impact on kids who'd never had anything new before. It helped make us a company that cared—not just on paper but in our employees' hearts.

The best business move

Although it wasn't our motivation, choosing to give back turned out to be a good business move. The public came into our stores based on what we did. We kept our sales messages separate from our community support, but prospective customers saw and liked what our dedication to foster kids said about our culture, about our company. We were told over and over again, "We shop at Sleep Train because of what you do for our community and foster kids."

It also had a difficult-to-measure but undeniable impact on our staff. Each drive improved how they felt about our company. They were proud to work somewhere that gave back and truly cared and they became even more dedicated to making a difference.

Giving back in your business

If your business doesn't already have a program in place to give back, you can take the lead in creating one. Start by choosing a cause that motivates you. There may be many areas that interest you and your colleagues, but focusing on just one cause will help you do more good than diluting your efforts into many areas.

Streamlining your philanthropy to one cause will also reduce the charity noise in your business. Being clear that you do give back and being able to state what your cause is gives you a reason to turn down requests for causes that do not match up with yours, with very little push back.

It doesn't really matter how you choose your focus area. I decided our company would support foster kids because of what I saw and due to a research paper on group homes I did in college, which gave me my first exposure to the subject of foster kids. You can make the executive decision as I did or you can solicit ideas from your leadership team or staff. No matter how you decide, my suggestion is to get started, stick to one, and learn as much as you can on how your company can best utilize the resources you have to help the cause.

Having one cause does not mean you and your employees can not still help other causes. It simply means that your company's financial support and focus is just in one place. We encouraged our employees to find their own cause, their passion, by giving them two paid days a year to work for a charity of their choice. We also created very effective team building events around helping other charitable organizations, while limiting our community drives, financial support, and requested vendor support to foster kids.

Brainstorm ways your company can use its unique position, products, or vendors to support your cause of choice, with or without a budget. As long as you never barter support for sales, whatever efforts you make will be a small step in the right direction to make a difference for those you support, your community and your company.

When you can't afford to give back

You may feel your company is not in a position to help right now. You might have challenging staff situations or be worried about your bottom line. It might feel like giving back is the last thing you should be concerned with right now.

But here's the hard truth: You will always have an excuse not to help *and* the ability to overcome those excuses. We all have money, time, or talent to give at one point or another. If you do not have money to give, there is always your time or your talents you can share. If you've been creative with your brainstorming, you'll have found manageable ways to give back to your community without jeopardizing productivity.

In fact, the sooner you start giving back, the faster you'll see employee retention improve, and your customer base become more connected to your brand. The more you give, the more you receive. I've seen this play out time and time again. The more we did to support foster kids, the more people supported our company. It's the classic chicken and egg situation; you can wait to improve your workplace before giving back, or you can give back and improve your workplace. I truly believe the latter is infinitely better.

You can do this no matter what stage your company is at. If you're just starting out or working up from difficult times, you don't need to jump in with both feet. You can start slowly and build up. The first thing our company gave was a bed. It was $100 at cost. At the time, that was a lot for my little store. Over the years we grew our company, expanded our efforts, and now I dedicate most of my time to the Ticket to Dream Foundation, reaching over 170,000 foster kids nationwide.

Find out more

If you want to find out more about how you can help foster kids in your area, check out our website at www.TicketToDream.org and search for programs in your state. There are many ways to help, from donating essential items to volunteering time, hosting fundraising events, becoming a foster or adoptive parent, mentoring foster kids, or simply donating online, and we'll get your money to our partners that are doing the best work. We work with over two hundred foster care services across the country and are growing rapidly.

We help great kids who've gone through a lot of trauma, and we give them opportunities to soar. It only takes one person to change a kid's life, and you could be that person.

I hope that wherever you choose to focus your efforts, you'll hold yourself accountable to giving back. It's simply the right thing to do.

A final word from Hernani

When I first heard about foster kids, I knew it was a bad situation. The stories tore at my heart. I recall a three-year-old girl and her five-year-old brother who were found by authorities in the backseat of a car. Both their parents had died overdosing on drugs in the front seat. As if that wasn't enough, when the kids entered the foster care system, they were separated. They only saw each other at summer camp.

My children are wonderful, but parenting even the best kids can be a challenge at times. Foster parents have kids who've been through intense trauma, and they take on all the messiness that comes with that. They need our support. I'm so thankful for our foster care system, and we can do more to help.

As one of Ticket to Dream's partners says, "Not everyone can be a foster parent, but anyone can help a foster child." We need to give back, and we need to hold ourselves accountable for doing so. I hope you'll join me.

♥ Take Action

1. Decide which charity your will company support and how you'll start giving back.
   Visit www.TicketToDream.org to learn more.

2. Schedule a time to discuss supporting a charity with your team or, if necessary, your superiors.

3. Email me at Hernani.Alves@BalancedIQ.com and tell me how your company will give back. I read every email, and we can hold each other accountable.

4. Take the Balanced Accountability eLearning transformation course that is personally taught by Hernani Alves and discover more tools to mastering Balanced Accountability.
   eLearning course at www.BalancedIQ.com

♥ Acknowledgments and UnConditional (UC) Love

My wife, **Angie** - I'm so grateful for the life we've created together. Many thanks for always being there for me and holding me accountable. UC

Carmina and **Riley** - You both continue to make me so proud, and I'm so blessed to have such amazing children. You know I love you unconditionally, and that's why I don't let you get away with things. Many thanks for holding me accountable as well. UC

My amazing parents, **Antonio** and **Maria Alves** - Your hard work, love, and accountability have blessed me with so many opportunities in life. UC

Frank and **Fatima Madruga** – Though you are my brother-in-law and sister, you both played a significant role in my life as my second set of parents. I'm blessed that you both held me accountable and guided me to becoming a better human being. Your confidence, love and support means so much to me. UC

My brothers, **Joe**, **Mario**, and **Michael** - For all your love, accountability, and support through the years. You have taught me so much, especially and always, family first. UC

Dale Carlsen - You're an amazing mentor and great role model. You have taught me so much on being a leader. I particularly thank you for listening to your father Paul's advice: "Surround yourself with great people, treat them well, and make everyone successful." UC

Tracy Jackson - I'm so thankful for all that you taught me, most importantly how to be a "human" leader. Even though I never met your father, Officer Friendly, I feel his presence in you every time we work together. UC

Matt Jessell – Feedback is a gift and I'm so thankful for you telling me what I needed to hear early on in my career. Many years ago, you were the first person to tell me to write a book. I apologize for saying you were crazy and there was no way I would ever do that. UC

My work wife at Sleep Train, **Matt Anderson** - We conquered so much, and I'm thankful for all our successful screw-ups together! I can't wait for our next successful screw-up. UC

Kyle Moore - It has been amazing to see your commitment and dedication to life since I first hired you at 16-years-old. I'm so thankful for all your feedback during this book journey. UC

Tammy Dudek - It has been so rewarding to see your leadership grow through the years. Many thanks for your guidance and feedback with the book. UC

Daniel Osuna - I was so fortunate to have you on my team. You always practiced what you preach. I apologize that you had to work with Hernazi, and I'm so glad that you witnessed my transformation into a better leader. UC

Scott Higgins - I loved all our time working together, and our strongest bond was unbreakable. Your leadership style is contagious, and you taught me that culture always trumps sales. UC

Brendan McGagin - Your story is an inspiration to so many and has catapulted you to success. Your dedication to always improving is a great example of a hero mentality. UC

Kenny Stivers - Your commitment to leadership continues to prosper. Many thanks for being on this journey with me. It's great to see you motivate and lead multiple teams throughout the country. UC

Liz Green - Many thanks for your extraordinary support and guidance with this book. I appreciate all that you did to bring this important leadership guide to fruition. I would not have been able to do this without you. UC

Natalie Macias and everyone that read each chapter that I've never met and offered great feedback - I appreciate all your advice and encouragement. UC

Foster care parents - This world is so blessed to have such caring individuals helping children. Your love and support is priceless. UC

A very wise man told me to always surround yourself with great people, I'm so blessed to have worked with so many amazing people during my career.

I love you all, Unconditional!

ABOUT THE AUTHOR

Hernani Alves is an entrepreneur, author, international speaker, and executive consultant with over twenty years of experience as a sales executive for a $3 billion company. He's the founder of Balanced IQ, a company that helps leaders build world-class teams and to get the results they desire. Hernani resides in California. Find out more at BalancedIQ.com.

Hernani is donating a portion of this book's proceeds to help foster kids get the support they need to thrive and create hope for a better tomorrow.

Speaker

Bring Hernani Alves to your next live event, podcasts, online summits, meetings or conferences. Hernani is a skilled presenter and trainer who brings a robust ability to convey what matters in a way that sticks. The audience will walk away with something real, something dynamic, and something that transforms their lives for the better.

To book Hernani as a speaker or coach, contact him directly: Hernani.Alves@BalancedIQ.com
www.**HernaniAlves**.com

Balanced IQ
Leadership